TELLING THE CHURCHES' STORIES

Telling the Churches' Stories

Ecumenical Perspectives
on Writing Christian History

Edited by

Timothy J. Wengert and
Charles W. Brockwell, Jr.

William B. Eerdmans Publishing Company
Grand Rapids, Michigan / Cambridge, U.K.

© 1995 Wm. B. Eerdmans Publishing Co.
255 Jefferson Ave. S.E., Grand Rapids, Michigan 49503 /
P. O. Box 163, Cambridge CB3 9PU U.K.

Printed in the United States of America

00 99 98 97 96 95   7 6 5 4 3 2 1

Library of Congress Cataloging-in-Publication Data

Telling the churches' stories: ecumenical perspective on writing Christian history /
    edited by Timothy J. Wengert and Charles W. Brockwell.
        p.   cm.
    Includes bibliographical references.
    ISBN 0-8028-0556-6 (pbk.: alk. paper)
    1. Church history — Historiography. 2. Ecumenical movement.
    I. Wengert, Timothy J. II. Brockwell, Charles W.
    BR138.T45 1995
    270'.072 — dc20   95-22023
                                             CIP

*This book is dedicated to Brother Jeffrey Gros,
Director of Faith & Order of the National Council
of Churches of Christ in the USA, 1981-1991.
His work is an inspiration on the ecumenical edge
of the ecclesia.*

Contents

Foreword

Justo L. González

Can church history be ecumenical? In many ways, both explicit and tacit, that is the question that this book explores. At some points, one hears tones of despair, as in the editors' references to the meetings in Burlingame in 1989. At other points, one encounters healthy skepticism as to the feasibility or even the desirability of the enterprise itself. And yet, the work that went into the fourteen principles of Christian history in ecumenical perspective shows that the issue is important and hopeful enough for a number of very busy scholars, historians, and theologians to spend years discussing it.

This question concerns me deeply, for I have devoted all my adult years to research, teaching, and writing on church history. And even long before that, I was committed to an ecumenical perspective.

In dealing with that question, historians, perhaps more than others, need to be reminded of José Ortega y Gasset's dictum: *la vida es gerundio, no participio* — life is a present participle, not a past participle. In the case of ecumenism, this means that there is no such thing as a "past-participle" ecumenism — one that is done, complete. Rather, ecumenism is always in the present participle — developing, emerging, discovering itself. And for us historians, it means that we must be humbled by the reminder that ours is an extremely fragile enterprise, as we seek to penetrate the past without leaving the present — that the "writing" of what "happened" is always a present-participle view of the past participle.

On the other hand, this enterprise, fragile and questionable as it is, is also enormously powerful. We use history to define ourselves, and we use it also to define others. History written in certain conflicting ways can lead to massacre in the Balkans. Historiography can ignore, and thus humiliate and almost obliterate, a people. And it can also bind a medley of nomad tribes into a people. History can liberate, and history can oppress. History can create, and history can destroy.

Thus, as more than one author in the essays that follow has indicated, the matter of an ecumenical perspective on church history involves moral values and theological options. I write this foreword as one who is convinced of the moral value of ecumenism, and who is committed to a theological outlook that undergirds that value.

Therefore, to the question, Can church history be ecumenical? I respond: no, it cannot; and yet, it must.

Church history cannot be ecumenical, because ecumenism is always in the present participle. Any rendering of church history that claims that it is already fully ecumenical is by definition sectarian — just as I would also argue that any theology that claims to be universal is by definition parochial and antiecumenical.

And yet church history must always be ecumenical, because a nonecumenical church is a contradiction in terms, because to tell the story of a part as if it were the whole denies the very essence of both the part and the whole.

How, then, does one go about writing this impossible yet necessary church history? Here one may distinguish between questions of scope and questions of perspective. And, since the matter of scope is the simpler of the two, at least on the surface, let us begin with it.

The matter of scope is most important in attempts to tell the whole of church history — that is, primarily in textbooks. As one of the contributors to this volume seems to suggest, in order to attempt such a global overview in these days of specialization, one must be either ambitious to the point of hubris or naive to the point of folly. (As someone who has undertaken such a task not once, but twice, I confess to both.) Yet this is a most important task, for it is through such textbooks that most emerging church leaders come to an understanding of their own history and of the history of the church whose servants and shapers they will be. Furthermore, I would argue that, precisely because ours is a time of specialization, such global overviews are significant even in shaping the views of professional historians in those areas that are not part of their own specialty.

As one compares textbooks written a few decades ago with those written with a more recent ecumenical perspective, it is clear that there has been a significant shift in scope. Most older textbooks were built in the shape of a pyramid. For instance, in the case of books written by Lutherans in the United States, in the earlier chapters both the Eastern and the Western branches of the church received due attention. As soon as one came to the Christological controversies and the councils of Ephesus and Chalcedon, the dissenting churches were ignored. Then, at some point around the Seventh Ecumenical Council, the East generally disappeared from view. In the sixteenth century, much was said about the Reformation, but nothing about the conquest of the Western Hemisphere or the expansion of Christianity into Asia. From that point on, Roman Catholics were generally ignored; and so were Calvinists, Anabaptists, and other sundry Protestants. At the peak of the pyramid, as the culmination of the entire historical process, stood the historian himself (generally, at that time, professional church historians were male) and his church. The result was that such a textbook was useful and used only among Lutherans, and did nothing to bring Lutheran readers to a better understanding and appreciation of the rest of the church catholic. More recent books, while not abandoning their particular stances — which in any case would be impossible — have a broader view of the church, and seek to bring to students a deeper understanding of other confessions and traditions. (A clear proof of this is that the most widely used textbooks are employed in Roman Catholic, "mainline Protestant," Pentecostal, Seventh Day Adventists, and many other seminaries and colleges.)

The widening of the scope of such books is also seen in their taking into account a wider gamut of Christian life and experience at various times and places. Although there is still much to be done, most textbooks in recent years have made an effort to take into account the differing experiences and the contributions of women, of the poor and the illiterate, of ethnic minorities, of practitioners of "popular piety," of members of churches that are not a part of the "mainstream" of Christian tradition, and so on. Obviously, this has been facilitated by the development and application of new methods of social studies to ancient texts and data; but what has given it an enormous impetus is the participation of these various voices in the current theological dialogue — once again, we are reminded that, although our subject is past participle, our enterprise is in the present participle.

The question of perspective is probably more significant than that of scope, for it affects every piece of historical research and writing, and not only those that seek to be as encompassing as possible. The very title of the chapter by the two editors of the present volume indicates the importance of this issue: "Christian History in Ecumenical *Perspective*."

Again, the very notion of "perspective" is indicative of trends toward the end of the twentieth century. Until fairly recently, to speak of a "perspective" in a supposedly objective enterprise such as "scientific" historiography would have been generally considered heresy. The goal of history throughout modernity was to achieve an objective description of the past — one that followed strict canons and could be equally verifiable by any rational human being.

Today, thanks to the postmodern criticism of modernity, we tend to be much more skeptical toward such claims. We know that any description of the past is to a great extent a social construct, one that says as much about the historian as it says about history.

While this certainly does not mean that there are no parameters to the discipline of history, it does mean that every historical account is perspectival — that it reads the past from the perspective of the reader.

This has important implications for our question. If by "ecumenical" we mean "universal," the quest for church history from an ecumenical perspective should be abandoned. Supposedly universal accounts are usually little more than an account written from a particular perspective that has the power to impose itself and that then suppresses all other accounts and perspectives as "partial" and not "universal."

There is, however, another way of looking at the "ecumenical." In this other sense, it implies the development of a general consensus in which particularities are still allowed to stand — not simply tolerated, but even welcomed — in the forging of a truly catholic consensus. In this consensus, particularities are never abolished. They are rather kept together by the bonds of the faith, much as the *different* four Gospels stand together, bound into a single canon, and yet irreducible in their differences.

In this sense, church history from an ecumenical perspective requires that historians recognize their own vantage points and lay aside any claim to a reading of the past apart from any particular vantage point. Any claim to the contrary — any account of church history that pretends to be universally valid, totally devoid of the writer's presuppositions — may turn out to be the most antiecumenical claim that a historian can make. At the same time a genuinely ecumenical church history may be one that unashamedly recognizes and proclaims its own perspective, acknowledges its own debt to myriad other equally partial perspectives, and then offers its own reading of the past as an offering to the ecumenical church at large.

As one of the writers in the essays that follow has indicated, growing specialization has made it increasingly difficult to write a universal account of the whole of the Christian story. This has been the trend for over a century, as more and more historical discoveries and new methods of inquiry have produced ever narrower specialties. But I suspect that in decades to come the real difficulty in such an attempt will come not from increased specialization, but from the growing awareness, even among the most stubborn "objectivists" in the field, that perspective always plays a role, and that the only way to prevent it from playing a noxious role is by acknowledging it.

In this humble acknowledgment of perspective, and in the consequent offering of every work as one that is partial and culturally bound, lies the future road for church history from an ecumenical perspective. I am gratified to see that characteristic in several of the essays that follow.

Preface

Timothy J. Wengert and
Charles W. Brockwell, Jr.

*That historians should give their own country a break, I grant
you; but not so as to state things contrary to fact. For there are
plenty of mistakes made by writers out of ignorance, and which
anyone finds it difficult to avoid. But if we knowingly write
what is false, whether for the sake of our country or our friends
or just to be pleasant, what difference is there between us and
hack writers? Readers should be very attentive to and critical
of historians, and they in turn should be constantly on their
guard.*[1]

As this reflection by Polybius reveals, the dangers of writing
history — for country, friends, or, we could add, church —
have been recognized and struggled with for at least two millennia.
This book continues to battle with some of the very difficulties Polybius describes, but in the context of the Christian churches of the
United States and their relation to both ecumenism and history. It
represents the efforts of the Apostolic Faith–History sub-working
group of the Working Group on Faith and Order of the National

---

1. Polybius, *History,* bk. 16.

Council of Churches of Christ in the USA, meeting during the quad-rennial from 1988 to 1991 to assess the impact of the writing of church history on ecumenism.

This work emerged from three paradoxes. The first centers in the fourteen principles for writing the history of Christianity from an ecumenical perspective.[2] These principles evolved over four years of meetings involving representatives from at least twenty-four churches, who began their work by reading together sections from the well-known textbook, originally by Williston Walker, *A History of the Christian Church*.[3] On the surface these fourteen statements appear plain and unexciting. That so many people could work so long on such principles may at first glance confirm every prejudice about committee work and multilateral ecumenical dialogues. Yet, when viewed from within the struggle echoed already by Polybius, these principles are no platypus. Instead they evince the difficulty of coming to terms with the impact of our views of church history on ecumenical theology and practice. They challenge us to reconsider the ways in which the writing of history may either foster divisions among the churches or, alterna-tively, obscure them. One member of the group, himself a church historian, spoke for all the participants in this project when he de-scribed how the work of the quadrennium had changed his approach to his own writing and research.

The struggle reflected in the origin of these principles points to a second, deeper paradox. At the meetings in Burlingame in March 1989, the minutes of the group reflected that "some members felt despair about the project, others pointed out that if ecumenical history is impossible, then ecumenism is also impossible." Historians, often dwellers in moldering archives or rarely used rare book rooms, may sometimes wonder whether their work has any impact, good or bad, on the larger issues facing the church. Students, forced by the un-yielding demands of seminary or university curricula to examine the detritus of such historical work, may also complain about the irrele-vance of such study. Yet these principles argue that how we write the

---

2. See chapter one.

3. Williston Walker, Richard A. Norris, David W. Lotz, and Robert T. Handy, *A History of the Christian Church*, 4th ed. (New York: Charles Scribner's Sons, 1985).

history of the Christian churches affects profoundly our ability to recognize one another's churches as either apostolic or catholic, to speak with one another about those things that divide us, or to assess the depth of our divisions or our unity.

From the belief that ecumenism and church history profoundly affect one another this book arose. The first section of this book, "Principles for the Ecumenical Writing of Christian History," reflects the conviction of the members of the Apostolic Faith–History sub-working group that these principles have no meaning outside of interaction with church historians and ecumenists. The first chapter, "Christian History in Ecumenical Perspective: Principles of Historiography," provides commentary by two members of the working group, the editors of this volume, who seek to place these principles within their appropriate church-historical and ecumenical contexts. They call upon historians of the church, ecumenical theologians, and the experience of the sub-working group itself, as well as the Scriptures and traditions of the churches themselves, to elucidate the difficulties of writing church history from this perspective.

This chapter with the fourteen principles was sent to two well-known scholars for their reactions. In chapter two Richard A. Norris, one of the collaborators on the fourth edition of Williston Walker's textbook, gives his own critical analysis of the principles in "The Fourteen Canons: Some Sidelong Critical Notes." His "puzzled but sympathetic" commentary provides a necessary critique of the principles, their moral basis, and the difficulties with their implementation. His closing comments on the problem and possibilities of fairness (cf. Principle 14) push the conversation between the historical guild and the churches to a deeper level.

The third chapter, "The Global Context of Ecumenical History," moves the conversation around these principles in a different direction. Drawing from his knowledge and experience of the worldwide ecumenical movement over the past four decades, Günther Gassmann places these principles squarely within the struggles toward increased unity by various churches during the twentieth century. He argues that the fourteen principles need to include a global, ecumenical perspective of Christian history, rooted in the church's tradition and unfolding in its own complex way within the recent history of Christianity. This added principle, when focused by the term "catholic," would provide the appropriate theological framework into which the principles could be applied.

These principles must withstand not only critical analysis but also daily use. For that they were sent to three church historians with the request that they contribute something to this volume from their ongoing scholarly work that would reflect their own ecumenical convictions and practice. Here these principles functioned not so much as disciplinarian (cf. Gal. 3:24) but as interlocutor (cf. Ps. 1), and the offerings of these scholars act as examples of what living with these principles might look like. From their work the second major section of this book, "Case Studies: Interacting with the Principles," arose.

The historians were chosen not merely on the basis of their abilities but also for their particular areas of expertise. Thus, case studies focus upon the Mediterranean churches of the fourth century, the central-European Reformation of the sixteenth century, and the American experience of the nineteenth and twentieth centuries for an immigrant church. A fourth historian, Professor David Daniels of McCormick Theological Seminary, contributed an oral report on an American-born church, the Church of God in Christ, and that church's particular worship practice of "tarrying." This study became, along with others, a portion of the consultation on American-born churches, held in Dallas, Texas, on March 13-14, 1991, under the auspices of the sub-working group.[4]

The ecumenical ramifications for these choices are clear. The Christological and Trinitarian debates of the fourth century, which led to the formulation of the Nicene Creed and the legal acceptance of the church in the Roman Empire, have had continuing impact on ecumenical conversations in the present.[5] Frederick Norris presents a

---

4. Dr. Daniels's contribution matches the focus of his doctoral work, "The Cultural Renewal of Slave Religion: Charles Price Jones and the Emergence of the Holiness Movement in Mississippi" (Ph.D. dissertation, Union Theological Seminary of New York, 1992), and was unavailable for publication in this book. See also his "Teaching the History of U.S. Christianity in a Global Perspective," *Theological Education* 29, no. 2 (Spring 1993): 91-112.

5. Mention need only be made of the continuing work by the Commission on Faith and Order of the World Council of Churches on the Nicene Creed and of the concomitant work of the Commission on Faith and Order on the national level. See especially Thaddeus D. Horgan, ed., *Apostolic Faith in America* (Grand

fresh look at Arianism in his "The Arian Heresy?" as a test case for the effect of theological controversy on the historical record and the churches' memory of it. How do ancient categories of heresy and orthodoxy influence our understanding of this crucial period in the history of Christianity?

The traumatic impact of events in sixteenth-century Europe continues to shape the ecumenical conversations of many churches, including those of the Anabaptist, Reformed, Lutheran, and Roman Catholic traditions. In "Katharina Schütz Zell: A Protestant Reformer," Elsie McKee uses the biography of an important but virtually unknown Protestant reformer of Strasbourg to uncover the complexities of urban church reform at the beginning of the sixteenth century and the remarkable fluidity of leadership within it. By resisting the temptation to reduce her to a type, McKee manages to unlock the distinctive qualities of this devout evangelical reformer for present readers.

On the American scene two kinds of churches, sometimes overlooked by historians, have exercised enormous influence in shaping Christianity in the United States: the immigrant church and the American-born church. American-born churches were the subject of a special consultation at which the participants analyzed a variety of churches, including the Nazarene, Wesleyan, Seventh Day Adventist, and Church of God in Christ. For this book James Hennesey has provided from the other grouping a look inside the mind and work of a Roman Catholic church historian and the difficulties that the American experience presents for writing history from his tradition and perspective.

Yet a third paradox of sorts lurks behind these two sections of this book. The fourteen principles, which gave rise to this book and the contributions described above, stand within a longer tradition within the ecumenical movement and yet, at the same time, provide a new perspective on these questions. In part this study arose out of

---

Rapids: Eerdmans, 1988). The importance of the fourth century for ecumenical dialogues is also demonstrated by another volume coming out of the Apostolic Faith–History sub-working group, *Faith to Creed: Ecumenical Perspectives on the Affirmation of the Apostolic Faith in the Fourth Century,* ed. S. Mark Heim (Grand Rapids: Eerdmans, 1991).

questions posed in the last triennium of the Commission on Faith and Order by the Apostolic Faith Study Group.[6] During that time (1985-87) those who worked closely on developing the volume *Apostolic Faith in America*[7] continually faced the difficulty of diverging, often competing, interpretations of the history of fourth-century Christianity in their work. This concern was further stimulated by the work of then director of Faith and Order Jeffrey Gros, who argued that the ecumenical movement needed some way of writing common accounts of church-dividing moments in Christian history in order to heal memories and indicate new possibilities toward developing a common identity within their diversity.[8] Gros in turn was motivated by the work of the Comision de Estudios de Historia de la Iglesia en America Latina (CEHILA) and by the discovery of another working group of Faith and Order studying the American context of the apostolic faith that large segments of American Christianity have been virtually ignored in theories about religion in America.

From these stimuli the work for the next quadrennium took shape, focusing particularly on the hermeneutical problems of writing church history from an ecumenical perspective. Work with the latest edition of Williston Walker's text began in this light. At the same time planning was underway for two consultations on a pair of issues that had already surfaced in the preceding triennium: the fourth-century churches and the American-born churches. As the principles took shape, these consultations also provided an important impetus for revising and refining the principles and the commentary on them. Examples of the ways in which these principles succeeded or failed in practice were abundant.

In chapter seven of this volume Thomas Finger, another member of the sub-working group, examines the work of our contributors and the broader interests of the Working Group on Faith and Order in light of the principles and reflects on the ways in which these principles

6. This historical section depends upon the work of O. C. Edwards, "The Ecumenical Church Historiography Project," *Ecumenical Trends* 21 (1992): 28-32.

7. See n. 5 above and Thomas Finger's more detailed discussion in chapter seven.

8. Jeffrey Gros, "Interpretation, History and the Ecumenical Movement," *Ecumenical Trends* 16 (1987): 117.

arose out of the greater ecumenical task. Here again the focus is not so much on criticism as on critical conversation and studied consideration. Finger demonstrates how the contributors to this book have interacted with the principles and how the principles might best work within a "corporately and ecclesially oriented" process. He also begins a process through which the contributors converse with one another.

Willy-nilly the group also discovered that it was part of a yet broader stream of interest in these ecumenical and historical issues. This is admirably demonstrated in Douglas A. Foster's "The Historiography of Christianity in Ecumenical Perspective: A Bibliographic Essay," chapter eight below. Not only the CEHILA project but also the World Council of Churches Commission on Faith and Order had already grappled with these issues.[9] But more than that, the concern for the relation between history and ecumenism was posed already in 1963 at the Fourth World Conference on Faith and Order held in Montreal, Canada, where the question of the relation between Tradition and the traditions became the center of controversy and agreement.[10]

Despite our debt to the Faith and Order movement both in this country and throughout the world, this study, by virtue of the way in which it developed, offers some surprising new voices for this discussion. For one thing it evinces a marked concern for the connection between church, gospel, and culture and for the often neglected voices from the history of the churches. For another, it has been fueled not simply by ecumenical considerations and theory but by a close, sympathetic, and yet critical reading of actual historical textbooks, notably

9. For details see Foster's essay.

10. See John Deschner, "A Brief Overview of the Faith and Order Movement (ca. 1910-1989) and a Brief Selection from Faith and Order Documents" (typescript, 1989), 36-38, citing P. C. Rodger and L. Vischer, eds., *The Fourth World Conference on Faith and Order (Montreal 1963)* (London: SCM, 1964). The document, "Scripture, Tradition and Traditions," section 3, paragraph 39, reads: "By *the Tradition* is meant the Gospel itself, transmitted from generation to generation in and by the Church, Christ himself present in the life of the Church. By *tradition* is meant the traditionary process. The term *traditions* is used in two senses, to indicate both the diversity of forms of expression and also what we call confessional traditions, for instance the Lutheran tradition or the Reformed tradition. . . [par. 40]. The concern of the second [part of the report] was with the problem of the one Tradition and the many traditions of Christendom as they unfold in the course of the Church's history."

that of Williston Walker. Third, it has been informed by the work of historians and theologians in the two consultations held during the quadrennium. Fourth, it has sought the participation of representatives from a wide range of both American-born and American-transplanted churches. Fifth, it has gone out of its way to seek the responses of church historians and ecumenists outside the working group itself. In this connection presentations of these principles were made at meetings of both the American Society of Church History and the American Theological Library Association, and articles were prepared for both *Ecumenical Trends* and *Fides et Historia*.[11] Finally, by giving the principles to "working historians" and letting them provide case studies developed while reflecting on these principles, this study underscores the difference between the church historian and those "hack writers" over whom Polybius frets. This volume invites both the readers of church history and its writers to be attentive, critical, and on their guard as we await that unity which comes only from the Holy Spirit through the Word.

11. See n. 6 and "Christian History in Ecumenical Perspective: Principles of Historiography," *Fides et Historia* 24 (1992): 40-53.

I. PRINCIPLES FOR THE ECUMENICAL WRITING OF CHRISTIAN HISTORY

1. *Christian History in Ecumenical Perspective: Principles of Historiography*

Charles W. Brockwell, Jr., and Timothy J. Wengert

Perhaps the two historical areas most likely to fall victim to party spirit are religious history and political history. Historians of Christianity are increasingly committed to applying to their specialty the same rigorous standards that govern other fields of *historia*. During the 1988-91 quadrennium of the Working Group on Faith and Order of the National Council of Churches of Christ in the USA, the Apostolic Faith–History sub-working group formulated fourteen principles for writing the history of Christianity from an ecumenical perspective as their contribution to the growing literature on ecumenical historiography.[1]

What follows are the fourteen principles developed by the group and the authors' commentary on them.[2] This commentary explains

1. The Apostolic Faith–History sub-working group, which comprised representatives from twenty-four churches (Protestant, American-born, Orthodox, and Roman Catholic) and which met biannually, was chaired by Professor Lauree Hersch Meyer, then of Bethany Theological Seminary, and Professor O. C. Edwards of Seabury-Western Seminary. For a discussion of the literature in this area see the bibliographic essay by Professor Douglas Foster that closes this volume.

2. For a description of the relation of this chapter to the development of the entire volume, see the preface.

the genesis of the principles and their place in the larger task of writing the history of Christianity.

The principles fall into five general categories: universality; context; commonality; particularity; and perspective. Those grouped under universality lift up those voices in the history of Christianity that historians have consciously or unconsciously excluded from their work. The second heading, context, emphasizes the interaction between gospel and culture and investigates the diverse sources for writing history from such a perspective. The third category, commonality, recalls the interplay between contemporary church-dividing or -uniting issues and the history of the churches. The fourth, particularity, reminds historians both how particular Christian voices and traditions may simultaneously judge and learn from other voices and traditions and what demands this particularity places upon the historians themselves. Finally, a fifth category, perspective, investigates hermeneutical considerations in the writing of history, as historians wrestle with prejudice and objectivity.

A. Principles of Universality

Principle 1: An ecumenical history of Christianity understands church history as the story of all who call themselves Christians, paying special attention to those Christians whose story has been ignored or suppressed.

> There is a correlation between the model of the church we hold and the way we approach church history. For a long time, the church has been identified with the clerical order and the history of the church has been understood as the history of the ecclesiastical institutions. . . .
>
> An important result of the modern ecumenical discussion is the rediscovery of the church as people and that the history of the church is necessarily, in the first place, the history of the people as subjects of their own history.[3]

3. T. V. Philip, "Church History in Ecumenical Perspective," in *The Teaching of Ecumenics,* ed. Samuel Amirtham and Cyris H. S. Moon (Geneva: WCC Publications, 1987), 45.

Ecumenical church history affirms a meaning of "church" much broader than any official denomination (as when persons ask, "What does the/your church teach?"), broader even than a wholly inclusive universal council of denominations. Ecumenical church history recognizes church wherever "two or three come together" in the name of Jesus (*sunegmenoi, congregati,* Matt. 18:20). Such a *synagogue,* such a *congregation* of those who acknowledge Jesus as "Lord and God" (John 20:28), "the Christ, the Son of the Living God" (Matt. 16:16), is an expression of *ecclesia,* part of the ecumenical story of all Christian people.

On the other hand, institutions like denominations and councils are also "church," for they too are "gathered in the name." (See "my church" *[mou ten ekklesian, ecclesiam meam]* of Matt. 16:18.) Any so-called history of the Christian people that scorns historic Christian institutions is as unecumenical as church history that includes only such phenomena as denominations and their designated religious persons.

Church history in an ecumenical perspective pays special attention to Christians whose story has been ignored or suppressed, making special efforts to see those usually overlooked (Luke 1:46-55) and to hear those usually thought to have no worthwhile story (Luke 7:36-50). "Dialogue with many of the movements outside . . . the ecumenical movement, is often not pursued because these groups are actually culturally despised, and it is unthinkable that critical theology would learn anything from dialogue with such sources."[4]

Principle 2: An ecumenical history of Christianity is global in outlook and seeks to avoid geographic centrism, classism, ethnocentrism, sexism, and the cult of personality.

From Genesis 1:1 to Revelation 21:1 the story of the people of God is set in the context of the first heaven and the first earth and the new heaven and the new earth. The city of God is for all nations (*ethnon, gentium,* Rev. 22:1-5; cf. Isa. 56:7; Mark 11:17; Acts 10:34-36). Election is not for privilege or dominance but for participation in God's work of reconciliation through love (Gen. 12:1-3; Mark 12:29-31; Luke 9:46-48; 2 Cor. 5:17-21).

Thus, for example, ecumenical church history seeks to go beyond

4. Donald W. Dayton, "Yet Another Layer of the Onion: Or Opening the Ecumenical Door to Let the Riffraff In," *The Ecumenical Review* 40, no. 1 (Jan. 1988): 88.

the stereotype of "normative home church shaping formative mission church" in the story of the growth of Christianity. Also, church history that is remembered ecumenically "turns the globe," so that every Christian faith community on the planet may fully display its reflection of the light of the gospel. "When the identity and the history of large groups of Christians are not recognized or [are] ignored, then the whole understanding of the universality of the church is completely distorted."[5]

The many names by which Christians are called (denominated) reveal the pluralism of Christian doctrine, spirituality, and polity. Pluralism that manifests rich diversity is healthy. But pluralism that condones division (*schisma, scissura;* 1 Cor. 1:10-15; 3:1-9; 11:18; 12) casts doubt on the credibility of God (John 17:20-23). Such institutionalized loss of the community of love and trust among disciples lacks scriptural warrant.

Whereas ecumenical church history affirms the diversity of the church and the need for various expressions of church, it sees the multiplicity of Christian communions in terms of complementing each other rather than competing against or correcting each other. Church history in an ecumenical perspective authenticates new moments in Christian history crystallized in the names and careers of persons who have "taught with authority." Often such moments have marked a stage in the progress of the pilgrimage of the people of God. Often movements that come to bear a *parteiisch* name are works of God. Yet, in ecumenical perspective every prophet is interpreted by his or her place among the whole people of God, not the catholic *ecclesia* evaluated by how closely it conforms to a denomination's heroic myth.[6] Inevitably, *parteiisch* is *parteilich.*

Principle 3: An ecumenical history of Christianity enables Christians to see and hear the full range of catholicity in the churches and to understand apostolicity in a variety of contexts. It also enables non-Christians to appreciate the great diversity of expressions of Christian identity.

5. Philip, 45. Our discussion concluded that Williston Walker et al., *A History of the Christian Church,* 4th ed. (New York: Charles Scribners' Sons, 1985), Period VII, Modern Christianity, is not ecumenical church history insofar as it centers in mainline, low church, USA Protestantism (COFO, AF/H, 3/89, MIN, 1).

6. "The pinch of salt or the touch of colour that finds its proportions only in the whole" (Dayton, 110).

Ecumenical church history distinguishes between "traditioning" (*accepi et tradidi*, 1 Cor. 11:23) and its historic (traditional) forms. The church historian who works ecumenically recognizes that "apostolic content" and "faithful continuity with the apostolic faith and mission" have varied doctrinal and institutional expressions (Luke 9:49-50).[7] The unbroken tradition of "the faith that was once for all entrusted to the saints" (Jude 3) is found in the continuous tradition of the saintly communities. Continuity in apostolic faith and content is not necessarily the same as historic continuity of institutional form.

Church history in an ecumenical perspective challenges the churches to acknowledge that "church" is their catholic identity rather than their denominational possession. This means that the churches are stewards (*oikonomous, dispensatores*, 1 Cor. 4:1), not proprietors, of the mysteries of God.

The ecumenical historian recognizes that the fullness of the body of Christ is not acknowledged in any single church by all other churches. While it is acknowledged that the full range of catholicity and apostolicity is to be found in the churches, it must also be admitted that the body of Christ is not yet built up to "unity in faith, . . . to the whole measure of the fullness of Christ" (*henoteta tes pisteos . . . tou Pleromatos tou Christou, unitatem fidei . . . plenitudinis Christi*, Eph. 4:12-13; cf. John 1-16).

B. Principles of Context

Principle 4: An ecumenical history of Christianity recognizes and investigates the interaction among gospel, communities of Christian faith, and culture.

---

7. *Baptism, Eucharist and Ministry*, "Faith and Order Paper No. 111" (Geneva: World Council of Churches, 1982), VI.53.a&b. Gustav Aulen and Anders Nygren have urged theologians to employ a principle of *Motivsforschung*, to see the essential Christian truth behind a doctrine rather than to stress the actual form in which it is presented. Thus the value of referring to the creeds as symbols. Scottish Free Church theologian James Denney is attributed with having said about creeds (and confessions?), "The best use to put them to is to sing them, rather than to sign them" (Edwin D. Mouzon, *Preaching With Authority*, Lyman Beecher Lectures on Preaching [Garden City: Doubleday, Doran, 1929], 225).

We can ignore neither the cultural context out of which the various churches have arisen nor their concomitant worldviews. The gospel does not speak into a vacuum, nor does it speak in words that the culture cannot understand or influence. Communities of Christian faith do not exist apart from the larger society or culture, but in relation to it. At the same time, these communities and their message cannot simply be identified with the surrounding culture.

Charles Norris Cochrane, in *Christianity and Classical Culture*, defines his task as a historian "simply to record those claims [to ultimacy by Christians] as an essential part of the historical movement which I have attempted to describe."[8] An ecumenical history of Christianity records the interaction between those Christian claims and the broader historical movement of which Christianity is itself a part.

To ignore this context could reduce Christian churches to disembodied ideals and would prevent their unique voices from being heard. It could also silence the voices from within the culture that challenge and interact with Christians and their message. It certainly would contrast sharply with the Christian Scriptures themselves, where, for example, one prophet anoints foreign kings (1 Kings 19) and another proclaims God's saving use of the Persian emperor, Cyrus (Isa. 45).

On October 25-27, 1989, the Apostolic Faith–History study group sponsored a consultation on fourth-century issues, entitled "From Faith to Creed."[9] A recognition of the importance of the interaction of culture and church in an ecumenical history of the church typified the consultation. There the participants focused upon the relation of creed, church, and empire. Different evaluations of the relation between *ecclesia* and *imperium* by participants from the various churches underscored the importance of this principle for writing ecumenical church history.[10]

Principle 5: An ecumenical history of Christianity takes into account the worship, piety, practice, and teaching of the various traditions, as well as doctrine, history, and institutional development.

We cannot reduce the history of the church to a history of ideas,

8. Charles Norris Cochrane, *Christianity and Classical Culture* (Oxford: Clarendon Press, 1944), vi.
9. S. Mark Heim, ed., *Faith to Creed* (Grand Rapids: Eerdmans, 1991).
10. COFO, AF/H4, 10/89, Statement, 2f.

liturgy, piety, or social and political involvement alone. From time to time, however, such narrow approaches have dominated the writing of church history either generally or in reference to certain eras or traditions. For example, several participants in the Apostolic Faith–History study group noted how one familiar Protestant account of the Christian church reduced the history of the Roman Catholic church in the nineteenth and twentieth centuries to papal decrees and actions.[11]

An ecumenical history of the church must portray the entire face of the church. This includes its "outward" face, as churches participate positively and negatively in their social, political, and cultural surroundings, but also its inward face, as churches pray, worship, bury, sing, celebrate important rites and sacraments, and reflect on their Scriptures and traditions. Such an ecumenical history would thus include both theology and practice. While traditional disciplines, such as the history of dogma, and newer disciplines, such as social history, will continue to demand separate attention by scholars, ecumenical history of the churches begins by recognizing the widest possible scope of Christian thought and practice as the basis for its work.[12]

This principle affects the shape of both the histories written and the primary materials collected and analyzed. Too often, for example, worship practices or piety have found little place in general treatments of church history. How effective or accurate a depiction do we sketch of a tradition when we concern ourselves only with its "great men" and their "great ideas" or, alternatively, with its "great social movements" and its "great political influence"? Without ignoring the institutions and doctrines that shape our churches, we must also record and remember our churches' spirituality. The great variety in genre, origin, and audience in the Hebrew Scriptures gives eloquent testimony to the range of sources and experiences historians of Christianity in other eras may also investigate.

11. See COFO, AF/H, 3/89, MIN, 1, and the pertinent discussion of Walker et al., 567-709.
12. In effect the revisers of Walker's text admit as much when they write, "Continuing historical research and methodological changes have led to important new discoveries and to fresh interpretations of the earlier periods, necessitating a much more thorough revision" (Walker et al., ix).

Principle 6: An ecumenical history of Christianity makes significant use of such sources as iconography, liturgy and worship, oral tradition, tracts and other popular literature, and the archeological record.

This principle supports the preceding two, inasmuch as it defines the context using the broadest possible range of historical data. In the past a narrow range of sources was used to reinforce the divisions of Christianity, rather than to serve as supports for understanding both unity and disunity. Different kinds of sources reveal more fully the richness of the Christian traditions and shed light on diversity in ways that may allow the divided churches to discover new approaches to unity.

This principle assists the historian in two ways. On the one hand, the broader the range of sources, the more accurate and engaging become the figures and events of the past. For example, Peter Brown in his biography of Augustine employs a stunning blend of archeological and written sources "to convey something of the course and quality of Augustine's life."[13]

On the other hand, very often nonliterary or obscure sources include information about groups and movements with which the historian would otherwise have no contact. Certain groups in the church, through either persecution or benign neglect, have no voice. Their writings may have been destroyed, or, as in the case of women, literary expression may have been denied to them. As important as theological "classics" from the past may be, the ecumenical historian ought not ignore or underestimate these other voices from the church's history, which may only find expression in its nonliterary artifacts. W. H. C. Frend demonstrates the enormous potential for such material in his reconstruction of the Donatist church.[14] More recently, Caroline Bynum has shown new ways to read historical texts to uncover the intense interaction between the social world and piety. Thus, she writes,

> My purpose in this book has been to put the behavior, the symbols, and the convictions of women and men in the distant past into their

13. Peter Brown, *Augustine of Hippo: A Biography* (Berkeley: University of California Press, 1967), 9.
14. W. H. C. Frend, *The Donatist Church: A Movement of Protest in Roman North Africa* (Oxford: Oxford University Press, 1985).

full context. Only by considering all the meanings and functions of medieval practice and belief can we explain medieval experience without removing its creativity and dignity.[15]

But Eusebius himself, by using documents of the Roman Empire, had already shown how a variety of sources may be used.[16]

C. Principles of Commonality

Principle 7: An ecumenical history of Christianity acknowledges that each generation and tradition reads the past in the light of its own lively issues.

No one can read earlier histories of Christianity without encountering the struggles of the historian's own church and time. Eusebius shaped his famous work to champion the harmony between Christian emperor and church.[17] Johannes Cochlaeus on the Roman Catholic side and Matthias Flacius on the Lutheran molded their histories of the Reformation to support their own partisan interests.[18] In the eighteenth century Gottfried Arnold used his "nonpartisan" history of the church to attack his orthodox Lutheran opponents.[19]

Contemporary issues also shaped one of the most influential

15. Caroline Walker Bynum, *Holy Feast and Holy Fast: The Religious Significance of Food to Medieval Women* (Berkeley: University of California Press, 1987), 298f.

16. See, for example, Eusebius, *The History of the Church from Christ to Constantine,* trans. G. A. Williamson (reprint; Minneapolis: Augsburg, 1975), Appendix E, "Sources Quoted or Summarized," 422-23. The Gospel according to St. Luke also reveals an interest in using a variety of sources (Luke 1:1-4).

17. For an evaluation of Eusebius's perspective see W. H. C. Frend, *The Rise of Christianity* (Philadelphia: Fortress, 1984), 477-79.

18. John Cochlaeus, *Commentaria . . . de actis et scriptis Martini Lutheri Saxonis* (Mainz, 1549). For a critical analysis of this work, see Adolf Herte *Lutherkommentare des Johannes Cochlaeus* (Muenster: Aschendorff, 1935); Matthew Flacius et al., *Ecclesiastica historia. integram Ecclesiae Christi ideam. . . .* (Basel: 1560-1574). The latter work is generally known as the *Magdeburg Centuries.*

19. Gottfried Arnold, *Unparteiische Kirchen- und Ketzer-Historie von Anfang des Neuen Testaments biss auf das Jahr Christi 1688* (Frankfurt am Main, 1700-1715).

histories of the Christian church published in the United States. In a brief conclusion to the first edition of *A History of the Christian Church,* published in 1918, Williston Walker writes,

> The long story of the Christian church is a panorama of lights and shadows, of achievement and failure, of conquests and divisions. It has exhibited the divine life marvelously transforming the lives of men. It has also exhibited those passions and weaknesses of which human nature is capable. Its tasks have seemed, in every age, almost insuperable. They were never greater than at present when confronted by a materialistic interpretation of life, and when the furnace of almost universal war bids fair to transform the whole fabric of European and American civilization. Yet no Christian can survey what the church has done without confidence in its future.[20]

Here Walker expressly reveals that both his theological assumption concerning the power of God and the evils of materialism and the historical context of the First World War have shaped his writing of this history. His words also indicate to us more than seventy years later a view of the world centered in Europe and the United States.

We acknowledge that in a similar way contemporary issues will continue to influence the writing of church history. Rather than denying their existence under the guise of a feigned objectivity, the ecumenical church historian must admit their importance and deal with them in a fair-minded way (see Principles 13 and 14). We discovered this principle at work in our consultation on the fourth century. As detailed below, historians from churches that had suffered persecution at some time in their past tended to emphasize concerns different from historians whose churches saw themselves in direct continuity with the conciliar process. At the same time, modern concern for liberation and feminist theologies has also shaped the kinds of issues considered important for the writing of ecumenical church history in the late twentieth century.

Principle 8: An ecumenical history of Christianity assists in the discovery of parallels in other times and places to contemporary concerns and reexamines divisive issues.

20. Williston Walker, *A History of the Christian Church,* 1st ed. (New York: Charles Scribner's Sons, 1918), 589.

In his article "Church History in Ecumenical Perspective," T. V. Philip makes the following plea.

> Ecumenical perspective means that historians must make the past alive and bring it to bear on the ecumenical issues and problems we face today. A number of the issues and problems we face today are not entirely new. Similar questions were raised in the past, though in different contexts and in different ways. We cannot completely identify past issues with those of the present and apply past solutions. Though not identical, some of the ecumenical issues being faced today have a striking similarity with some of the issues faced by the church earlier.[21]

His analysis makes two things clear. First, ecumenical church history is not history for its own sake, but for the sake of shedding new light on issues dividing Christians today. Second, although past events are not identical with present circumstances, nevertheless their similarities to our own times make them worthy of our attention.

Thus, the church historian holds up the mirror of history to the churches and encourages them to find some reflection of themselves in what took place. In the light of such a discovery the churches can confess that what they are experiencing has in a similar way been experienced by Christians in the past. This solidarity with the past may enable churches to use their history as a witness to the unity we seek in Jesus Christ.

To be sure, identity with the past can also be used in church-dividing ways. However, especially in a world where the term "distant past" implies to some anything that occurred more than fifty years ago, we neglect the history of Christianity at our own peril. Ignorance of that history may doom the churches to repeat mistakes of the past.

Nowhere has renewed interest in the historical sources contributed to changes in ecumenical relations more clearly than in the history of the Reformation. For example, progress made in bilateral

---

21. Philip, 50. He cites examples of the relations of Jews and Gentiles in the earliest church and the struggle between Catholicism and Donatism in the fourth and fifth centuries.

conversations between Lutherans and Roman Catholics in the United States has always been accompanied by renewed examination of the historical sources on both sides.[22] Similar examples could be gathered from relations among other churches as well.

As we found out in our consultation on the fourth century, discovering parallels to the past can also continue old divisions. On occasion, participants imported experiences from other periods of the church's history into their interpretation of that century. As the summary statement describes it:

> Christian groups who have experienced persecution and domination at the hands of other Christians in control of political power sometimes read the fourth century in terms drawn from these experiences. Churches that regard themselves as in direct continuity with the conciliar process that formed the [Nicene] creed tend to see the fourth century through the model of development toward the fully realized structures and theology that came afterwards.[23]

But even this awareness, which also arises from an honest assessment of our various histories, can assist the process of reinterpreting such issues.[24]

D. Principles of Particularity

Principle 9: An ecumenical history of Christianity assists groups of Christians to define their own voices within the conversations among

---

22. See, for example, the background papers in H. George Anderson et al., eds., *Justification by Faith: Lutherans and Catholics in Dialogue VII* (Minneapolis: Augsburg, 1985), 111-315. On the same issue, from the Roman Catholic perspective, is the collection of articles edited by Jared Wicks, *Catholic Scholars in Dialogue with Luther* (Chicago: Loyola University, 1970). A similar use of the historical data marks the Reformed/Lutheran bilaterals as well. See Paul C. Empie and James I. McCord, eds., *Marburg Revisited: A Reexamination of Luther and Reformed Traditions* (Minneapolis: Augsburg, 1966).

23. COFO, AF/H4, 10/89, Statement, 2.

24. The same process of reinterpretation of the present on the basis of the past may be seen in the powerful effect that the reading of the law had on Ezra's hearers in Nehemiah 8–9.

communities of faith and to issue their special challenge to these communities.

As early as the first generation of the church we discover varieties of ways of being the church, with the resulting tensions such mutual challenges create (Acts 15; Gal. 2). While they may no longer be insuperable obstacles to *communio in sacris,* differences in polity are significant because they reflect differences in ecclesiology. "Polity is the shape of our corporate obedience."[25] Church history in an ecumenical perspective respects the histories that have given rise to so many different Christian polities. Faithful women and men have both paid and exacted a high price in their loyalty to their understanding of the meaning of church.

Ecumenical historiography enables churches to be secure in their resilient core identity while acknowledging the apostolicity and the apostolates of other Christian communities. A triple effect of the past century of ecumenical dialogue has been greater knowledge of one's heritage, greater confidence in one's mission, and greater openness to and affirmation of other communions. In ecumenical church history "other" does not imply "alien" (John 10:16).

This is illustrated by a 1970s project of the Lutheran Institute for Ecumenical Research on "The Identity of the Lutheran Churches in the Context of the Challenges of Our Time." "All reflections on what is specific about Lutheran churches, Lutheran confession, Lutheran piety or Lutheran ethos by no means should hide the fact that here, too, the primary object is the realization of the church of Jesus Christ, of Christian confession, Christian piety and Christian ethos. . . . But at the same time it also became evident that — almost as a matter of course — this Christian identity is lived out and becomes reality in the form of confessional, that is Lutheran, identity."[26]

The process of becoming articulate within the conversations among communities of faith soon involves a church in its own intramural practice of ecumenical historiography. Voices silenced or ignored within a communion have a chance to make themselves heard and to be taken seriously. Thus, the churches learn more about them-

25. Attributed to United Methodist Bishop Wayne Clymer.
26. *Lutheran Identity* (Strasbourg: Institute for Ecumenical Research, 1977), 53.

selves and discover that "a richly textured historical identity can create
a new world because it reveals something about ourselves that we did
not know."[27] Church history in an ecumenical perspective gives the
churches an opportunity to grow into the New Testament ideal of
unity in Christ Jesus that transcends barriers of ethnicity, class, or
gender (Gal. 3:28).

Principle 10: An ecumenical history of Christianity opens each
particular tradition to critical analysis by others.

"But we have this treasure in clay pots to show that this all-sur-
passing power is from God and not from us" (2 Cor. 4:7). Paul's
personal reference applies to churches as well. Churches often confuse
the clay with the treasure. Some assert that their clay pot contains all
the treasure, for them to dispense as they choose. At times churches
act as if other communions have only a few trinkets that can in no
way add materially to their great treasury. Some Christian communities
have assumed theirs was the only — or at least the best — design for
the clay pot.

Church history in an ecumenical perspective allows the churches
to take pride in their coining of the treasure of the gospel and requires
them to exercise humility in learning how others look upon their clay
jar. Church historians who work ecumenically care about Christian
communities other than their own and strive for empathetic dialogue
with them.

Principle 11: An ecumenical history of Christianity welcomes
people to investigate with the historian the Christian past in a spirit
of hospitality.

Scriptural hospitality *(philoxenia, hospitalitas)* is the entertain-
ment of the stranger or sojourner as a guest (Gen. 18:18; 19:1-11;
Isa. 58:7 [although the word does not appear in the Hebrew Scrip-
tures]; Matt. 25:35; Rom. 12:13; Heb. 13:2; 1 Pet. 4:9). "Hospitality
was the chief bond which brought the churches [of the Mediterranean
basin in New Testament times] a sense of unity."[28]

27. Donald G. Mathews, "Women's History/Everyone's History," in
Hilah F. Thomas and Rosemary Skinner Keller, eds., *Women in New Worlds:
Historical Perspectives on the Wesleyan Tradition,* vol. 1 (Nashville: Abingdon,
1981), 29.

28. V. H. Kooy, "Hospitality," in George A. Buttrick, ed., *The Interpreter's
Dictionary of the Bible,* vol. E-J (Nashville: Abingdon Press, 1962), 654.

In this context of church history in ecumenical perspective the stranger is the historian from one communion who hesitates to speak about the story of other churches. The stranger here is also the Christian who, untrained in the skills of the professional historian, is reluctant to investigate the past with historians. Likewise, the stranger is the non-Christian historian whose research must take account of the historic role of Christian ideas and institutions. Sojourners in strange Christian faith communities are to be welcomed for their perceptions of home traditions different from their own. Strangers to the historian's craft are to be welcomed for insights into what nonspecialists think about what constitutes church and mission. Historians from outside the Christian faith community altogether are to be welcomed for their appraisal of how Christianity has affected history. The spirit of hospitality demonstrates openness to critical analysis by others.

Practicing hospitality in doing church history is also one of the "ways to track the story of the internal nature of churches, of their day to day piety — the story of their spirituality, not the story of institutions."[29] The sojourner in this relationship listens to the passions and commitments of the other(s) stated from their point of view. "The sense of getting inside a tradition involves the [guest] in the passion of what is being studied. The part of me touched by what touches those in another tradition involves me with their insight into their spirituality, helps me realize I'm partaking of the same life-giving breath of God." This is "approaching church history as a conversation of peoples of faith."[30]

Principle 12: An ecumenical history of Christianity approaches its task in the spirit of repentance and forgiveness, avoiding defensiveness with regard either to social location or to particular theological, methodological, or ecclesial traditions.

Church history in an ecumenical perspective makes "every effort to keep the unity of the Spirit through the bond of peace" (*eirenes, pacis,* Eph. 4:3). Two international dialogues of the past decade illustrate this principle. "We are aware that we come from two very different Christian backgrounds. Our histories, our cultural journeys, our theological traditions and methods have, in some often important

29. COFO, AF/H, 3/89, MIN, 1.
30. COFO, AF/H, 3/89, MIN, 1-2.

respects, been different. Some of the problems between us spring from these differences." "From the beginning we were determined, in accordance with our mandate, and in the spirit of Phil. 3.13, 'forgetting what lies behind and straining forward to what lies ahead', to discover each other's faith as it is today and to appeal to history only for enlightenment, not as a way of perpetuating past controversy."[31]

The ecumenical search for Christian history is possible only through humility about one's own tradition combined with respect for all others who "gather in the name" of Christ Jesus.

E. Principles of Perspective

Principle 13: An ecumenical history of Christianity seeks to understand and clearly to acknowledge its own presuppositions and seeks to overcome its prejudices.

The task outlined in this principle stands under the command of Jesus Christ in Matthew 7:1-5. Commenting on these verses, Eduard Schweizer argues that "Jesus himself probably intended radical liberation from all categories to which we would assign others and above all ourselves."[32] An ecumenical history of Christianity can seek to do no less. Failure to do so would blind such work with the massive beams and logs human beings eagerly overlook in their zeal to judge others.

Among other places, historians may rightly acknowledge their limitations in the prefaces or afterwords to their own works. In this spirit Clyde Manschreck begins his history of Christianity with a chapter entitled "Presuppositions and the Beginnings of Christianity." After stating that the history of Christianity is "*one* record of how agape has been received, what it has meant, and what it may mean for contemporary man," he concludes

31. *Apostolicity and Catholicity: Report of the Disciples of Christ–Roman Catholic International Dialogue,* First Series 1977-1982 (Indianapolis, IN: Council on Christian Unity, 1982), 2; Anglican–Roman Catholic International Commission, *The Final Report* (London: SPCK, 1982), 1-2.

32. Eduard Schweizer, *The Good News according to Matthew,* trans. David E. Green (Atlanta: John Knox Press, 1975), 170.

The above is, of course, a confessional, presuppositional stance that has many ramifications. While such presuppositions are acknowledged, the author does not seek to make them obtrusive, nor does he seek to propagandize, but various interpretations and evaluations of the history of Christianity will reveal that they are there. Good scholarship and all that these two words connote in terms of relative objectivity, documentary and source evidence, and reasonable substantiation of observations will be attempted. But no one escapes his own time.[33]

Principle 14: An ecumenical history of Christianity acknowledges that no historical account can claim complete objectivity, but seeks fair-minded empathy with the particular stories that comprise the ecumenical history of the Christian people.

This principle touches upon certain philosophical issues that go far beyond the scope of this analysis.[34] Nevertheless, it raises two important points. On the one hand, the writer of an ecumenical history cannot claim complete objectivity. This is not possible because the events under investigation are irretrievably fixed in the past the moment they occur. Moreover, the memory of these events and the historian's analysis of them bear all the marks of the struggles and limitations of our common humanity.

On the other hand, this principle calls historians of the church to "fair-minded empathy." This means that in writing the church's story the historian embarks upon a continuous conversation with the sources and with other historians, past and present, in an effort to allow the churches' memory of things said and done to come to life through balanced research and analysis. This includes a careful hearing

33. Clyde L. Manschreck, *A History of Christianity in the World: From Persecution to Uncertainty* (Englewood Cliffs, NJ: Prentice Hall, 1974), 5. Manschreck's own use of what is now labeled noninclusive language verifies his final point.

34. A classic analysis of this problem is found in Carl Becker, "Everyman His Own Historian," *American Historical Review* (Jan. 1932): 221-36. See also Jerald C. Brauer, "Changing Perspectives on Religious History in Context," in *Reinterpretation in American Church History,* ed. Jerald C. Brauer (Chicago: University of Chicago Press, 1968), 1-28 and 195-218 respectively, cited in William Dean, *History Making History: The New Historicism in American Religious Thought* (Albany: State University of New York Press, 1988), 68-70.

of those voices both inside and outside of the church that are often excluded or marginalized.

In an attempt to define this mode of doing history, participants in the Apostolic Faith–History study group used phrases such as "hearing the past in its own terms," "a situated objectivity," and history as "a reflective process." They stressed the importance of "humility and confession," warned against becoming enraptured by the power and glory of heroes and heroines, and finally encouraged the writing of "history that is open, hospitable to the reader."[35] Despite its obvious "slant" toward the subjects of its history, the Acts of the Apostles itself may in some ways demonstrate the empathy that participants in the study group sought to describe.

Conclusion

The lament of Robert Burns, "Oh wad some power the giftie gie us, to see oursels as others see us," must be written on the lintel of any essay dealing with this subject. The participants in this study group share a deep concern for the disunity of the church and a conviction that reexamination of the historical record continues to serve a crucial function in continuing efforts at ecclesiastical rapprochement. Despite the wide range of traditions represented, there remained the sense that among the missing voices around the table were those representing some of the more conservative points of view. Moreover, we were all professional, university-trained men and women, predominantly of European ancestry. For all the strengths that such experience and education endow, they can also make it difficult for us truly to comprehend and express the concerns of others differently educated and with different cultural locations. Our concerns to include those traditionally marginalized and to approach history writing in a fair-minded way may, in the eyes of some not privy to our deliberations, lead instead to an unfair marginalization of precisely that gospel which Christians hold dearest. It is under this burden that historians of the Christian movement must always operate.

35. COFO, AF/H, MIN, 10/89, 2-3. For the last two points (confession and hospitality), see Principles 11 and 12 above.

2. The Fourteen Canons:
Some Sidelong Critical Notes

Richard A. Norris

The observations that follow are intended as a sort of running — and puzzled but sympathetic — commentary on the fourteen principles that are being set out here in an attempt to define the character and qualities of an "ecumenical" — that is, global and inclusive — "history of Christianity." I have chosen this format both because it seems to fit the personal character of these remarks and because it reflects fairly accurately the winding and uncertain course that my thinking about them has followed. It seems to me, in the end, that they mix methodological and moral questions in a somewhat confusing way and that, for all the soundness of the attitudes they commend, they fail to suggest what the special contribution of historians might be to a thoroughly ecumenical grasp of the character of the Christian movement, perhaps because they are — unlike your average, workaday historian — more focused on the present than on the past.

I.

1. An ecumenical history of Christianity understands church history as the story of all who call themselves Christians, paying special attention to those Christians whose story has been ignored or suppressed.

The phrase "an ecumenical history of Christianity" is an odd one. Obviously it wants to commend history written in an ecumenical spirit — that is, a spirit that is fair to all the currents, marshes, eddies, vortices, and puddles that have been created by the moving river of shared Christian faith and life. The expression "an ecumenical history," however, does not convey this thought very clearly. What is more, as the rubric "universality" suggests, one is more likely to take it to denote a piece of historical writing that aspires to give an account of the whole of the Christian story. But interpreted in this sense, the canon would have limited usefulness, since it would not apply to the great majority of works written in the field of church history.

Few writers, after all, in this age of specialization, would even attempt such an enterprise, unless they had been persuaded by the prospect of significant royalties to pen a textbook or an illustrated guide; and those — like the present writer — who have been part of such an attempt are prone to be more conscious than others of the degree to which considerations of space and of relevance to one's likely readership dictate what might euphemistically be called "selective emphasis." A history of Christianity that is intended largely if not exclusively for a Roman Catholic or Protestant audience in North America, and that prudent editors limit to a single volume, is unlikely, even if printed in small type, to do real justice to the history of churches in, say, the Greek, Slavic, Syrian, or Egyptian traditions. Conscience may dictate that significant mention be accorded them; but conscience may also wonder whether significant mention is not sometimes more insulting than silence. In any case, books of this sort are relatively few; their readership is limited; and they are normally — and rightly — regarded as elementary. Most professional historians eschew the writing of such works and confine themselves to articles and monographs of one sort or another; and the question is therefore bound to arise whether the phrase "ecumenical history" can realistically be applied to the great majority of the literature that is written about the Christian movement.

Further, the use of the term "Christianity" and of the expression "church history" raises a question about the subject matter of this particular historiographical enterprise. "Christianity" is a manifest abstraction, and an abstraction that is difficult to define. (Would one, for example, accept as a definition of "Christianity" the Christological and Trinitarian criteria specified by the World Council of Churches as requisite marks of its member bodies? What effect would this have on the scope of "ecumenical history"?) Similarly, the word "church" in the expression "church history" would seem, in the end, to require theological definition. Perhaps it would be better to employ a phrase like "the Christian movement," which seems somewhat more non-committal, more capable of phenomenological definition, and more consonant with the intent of the expression "all who call themselves Christians."[1]

I wonder, therefore, whether it might not be better to say: "Historians who write about the Christian movement in an ecumenical spirit understand that their aim is, in principle, to construct the story of any and all who have called themselves Christians, and they pay special attention to groups whose story has been ignored or suppressed." It would have to be said, though, that even this phrasing of the principle does not make it easily applicable to authors of monographs, unless it be interpreted simply as encouragement for scholarly concentration on neglected periods or movements; and given the normal pressures of academic existence, this is not a species of encouragement for which there exists a crying need.

2. An ecumenical history of Christianity is global in outlook and seeks to avoid geographic centrism, classism, ethnocentrism, sexism, and the cult of personality.

This statement is best read, I think, as an illustration of Principle 7: that is, it specifies a set of "issues" that happen to be "lively" for the current generation of academics, and especially, perhaps, western academics. It has, therefore, a certain paradoxical quality, in that its call for a historiographical practice that is "global in outlook" requires that it assign a position of privilege to the intellectual agenda of a

---

1. Perhaps this is an allusion to the language of Archbishop Cranmer: "all who profess and call themselves Christians" (see the American Book of Common Prayer [1928], 18). If so, it may intimate a distinction, not without usefulness to the historian, between the visible and the invisible church; though this distinction is not as popular with theologians as it once was.

particular era. It proposes, in fact, to practice temporal, as distinct from spatial or geographical, "centrism." This circumstance suggests that "globality" (if that is a licit word) functions more to designate a hope than it does to name an "outlook" that any individual or group could be expected or required to possess. Indeed one wonders whether, in at least one range of its connotation, the phrase "global in outlook" is not roughly synonymous with that "complete objectivity" which "no historical account can claim" (Principle 14; and see 1 Cor. 13:9f).

If this is *not* the case, then one would have to suppose that the phrase refers, as Principle 13 puts the matter, either to a presupposition to be acknowledged (in which case Principle 2 must be taken as such an acknowledgment) or to a prejudice to be overcome. In the latter circumstance, Gadamer's reflections, in *Truth and Method,* on the hermeneutical utility of prejudice might be pondered to good effect.

Indeed I wonder whether Principle 2 might not better be turned on its head and rephrased as a defense of the vast variety of prejudices, presuppositions, and interests that necessarily inform historical study and writing. Feminist treatments of Christian history can scarcely be labeled "global in outlook"; yet none would deny their utility or their ability to bring forgotten tracts of history to light. Neither the J Document, nor recent studies of black religion in Africa and the Americas, nor the new birth of Latin American church history can be acquitted of a certain "ethnocentrism"; and for that matter, the Acts of the Apostles, with its Jerusalem-to-Rome axis, arguably suffers from "geographic centrism." If the fourth-century Arian historian Philostorgius were with us, it would doubtless be necessary to add "homoousianism" to the above list of forbidden delights. But why forbid them if they contribute to knowledge and understanding? One of the unvarying characteristics of cutting edges in academic research is to be narrow.

Perhaps, then, "globality" of outlook needs to be redefined to some extent. For one thing, it needs, I think, to be made clear that what is being recommended is not a method but a *moral* attitude, at whose heart there lies not a pretense to objectivity but a commitment to even-handedness or fairness. Such a commitment would entail at least three policies. In the first place, it would call historians to admit the necessity of a wide range of prejudices and prepossessions, with the particular questions, perspectives, and methods they engender, to the writing of history — and this despite, if necessary, current hermeneutical fashions and orthodoxies. Consequently, in the second place, it would call individual historians to abate to some reasonable degree the exclusivity with which they commend the methods and perspectives they themselves happen to espouse, and thus not merely to make space for other approaches but even to weigh, seriously if critically, the latter's results. And finally, it would call historians to confess *(homologein!)* that whatever "wholeness" an account of the past can lay claim to derives from the patient and critical attempt, ever renewed, to weigh the results of a multitude of inquiries and fit them together into some sort of reasonably proportioned picture. The latter task, it must be admitted, is exceedingly difficult and, at least nowadays, seldom undertaken. The enterprise of synthesis is not favorably regarded by dissertation or tenure review committees.

3. An ecumenical history of Christianity enables Christians to see and hear the full range of catholicity in the churches and to understand apostolicity in a variety of contexts. It also enables non-Christians to appreciate the great diversity of expressions of Christian identity.

I do not know exactly what "catholicity" and "apostolicity" are meant to connote in this particular statement, though it seems they are intended to signify different aspects of the "Christian identity" referred to in the second sentence. Nevertheless I would be prepared to affirm that, whatever qualities or characteristics these words refer to here, such qualities or characteristics occur in Christian bodies that are, in other respects, very different from one another.

   If, then, there is a problem with this statement, it does not lie in the substance of what it seeks to say: diversity and family resemblance not infrequently go hand in hand. There is a problem, though, in the bland assumption that histories of Christianity — and especially perhaps one-volume textbooks — are in fact extensively read, whether by ordinary "Christians" or by ordinary "nonbelievers," and therefore that the discipline called church history serves an audience much wider than that which consists of church historians themselves, church historians in training, and seminary students. As far as I have been able to observe, one does not often find histories dealing with the Christian movement in any save seminary bookstores or bookstores exclusively devoted to religious matters (which are themselves few and far between); and if one does, they tend not to be written by professionals. What would have to happen to the writing of Christian history (or, for that matter, any other sort of history) to rescue it from its obscure corner in the cloisters of academe? That would be a question worth addressing in such a document as this.

II.

It is not clear to me that the three principles that follow — under the general rubric of "context" — are all of a piece. What they have in common is an intent: to extend the principle of globality or ecumenicity so that it governs not only the historian's notion of what constitutes "church," but also his notion of what goes into the making of an acceptable portrayal of the past of the Christian movement. Thus, the first (Principle 4) is addressed to the problem of the Christian movement's relation to culture (and society?) in its several historical settings. The second (Principle 5), however, appears to name two sets of factors in, or aspects of, the life of Christian groupings and to weigh their importance as foci for historical inquiry. I do not see, though, that either set can be taken as providing the *context* of the other. Principle 6, finally, treats of types of evidence that may be available to the historian of a particular era; and while its exhortation to inclusiveness or catholicity in the use of these "sources" is unexceptionable, it is surely a mistake to confuse *evidence* with context. The remarks that follow, therefore, treat these principles as addressing separate issues.

4. An ecumenical history of Christianity recognizes and investigates the interaction among gospel, communities of Christian faith, and culture.

It is certainly wrong — indeed I would say impossible — to focus on the story of the Christian movement (or anything else), in any of the many times and places in which it has appeared, without reading it in the light of a context that renders its practices and teachings intelligible. Such a context can best be likened, I think, to a language — the language whose rules, habits, and idioms must be presupposed in assessing the sense of a particular utterance. Furthermore I would agree that the term "culture" — so long as it is understood to encompass the evolving social roles, practices, and institutions in which a cultural "mind" is embedded — serves nicely to indicate the sort of thing that "context" means in this connection. A culture is, after all, a kind of language, but a language that includes behaviors, with the beliefs and attitudes embedded in them, as well as speech; and this remains the case even if cultures, like languages in the narrow sense, are always in motion, like the swirling cloud formations that accompany a storm.

Principle 4, however, seems to me to be evasive in two respects. First of all, it does not specify which of the many available cultural contexts it has reference to. Whatever may be the case with the relics of saints in the dimension of space, the relics of history, the materials that the historian interprets, suffer from multiple location in the dimensions of time and culture. They are readable — and are read — in any number of contexts. I am myself entirely sympathetic with the view that the historian (whatever other folk may choose to do) has an obligation to privilege the *original* cultural and social setting of any particular set of the past's leftovers. This is, after all, a matter of mere fairness to the authors of the words or actions one is attempting to understand. To carry out this undertaking, however, is, as they say, a neat trick. To understand a set of doings and thoughts carried through in one cultural language while employing as one's predestined tool another such language is a business of great delicacy and difficulty, which occasions for historians (or ought to) much doubt, hesitation, and even, occasionally, fits of despair. It will not do, then, simply to *command* such an undertaking, when the difficult question is how — and even whether — the command can be obeyed.

These remarks, however, suggest a second way in which Principle 4 is evasive. If on the one hand contextual location is an indispensable condition of historical interpretation, and if on the other the word "culture" frames roughly what one means in this case by "context," one is bound to ask what is meant by "the interaction among gospel, communities of Christian faith, and culture." The term "interaction" suggests that the three items named are in principle independent of one another: that one might conceivably isolate (this particular) gospel from (these particular) committees of faith, and the latter from (this particular) culture. Only so, it would seem, does it make sense to speak of their "interaction." Yet the rubric "context" would appear to assign a certain priority to culture here: that is, to suggest that Christian communities and their "gospel" are more parts or facets of their culture than they are independent interactors with it.

For all that, there is an obvious plausibility to this talk of "interaction." I for one doubt whether the sort of thing "gospel" denotes can subsist independently of *some* community. On the other hand, a continuing community may be — and indeed to some extent inevitably is — the bearer of a (sub-)culture that to some degree differentiates itself from the culture of a larger society. Such seems to have been the situation of the Christian movement in the world of late antiquity; and such seems to be its situation now. This suggests, however, not only that the relation or "interaction" between the culture of the Christian movement and that of the society in which it is set may take different forms in different times and places, but also — and for present purposes more significantly — that even in their original historical locations the data of Christian history can often legitimately be read in at least two contexts. There is that of the "mind" or (sub-)culture perpetuated by the continuing life of Christian communities, and that of the "mind" or culture of an encompassing social grouping. Thus, the question might arise as to which of these contexts is primary. Does one read the history of Christianity in India as part of "church history" or as part of the ongoing story of Indian culture? Does one read the history of Christianity in the late antique world as continuing the story of Jerusalem or that of Athens and Rome — or both, or neither? This issue — a fairly burning one in practice — probably has no simple or straightforward answer; but in any case it should not be glossed over, in the interest of "globality" or "ecumenicity," by tacitly identifying "culture" with "context," and that in turn with the operative tradition or mind of society-at-large as contrasted with that of the Christian community or communities. There must be some sense in which the study of Christian history is different from the study of absolutely everything.

5. An ecumenical history of Christianity takes into account the worship, piety, practice, and teaching of the various traditions, as well as doctrine, history, and institutional development.

Of all the principles in this list, I find this one the most obscure. For one thing, the language itself is equivocal. What is the difference between "teaching" in the first set of topics and "doctrine" in the second? And if "ecumenical history" is the umbrella under which both sets of topics are ranged, what does the word "history" denote in the second of the two sets? Finally, I do not see that the topic "institutional development" can be reasonably interpreted in a way that excludes such phenomena as worship and piety — though this may represent an idiosyncratic view.

More substantively, it is not entirely clear, at least to me, what issue is being addressed. The phrase "as well as" seems to imply that "doctrine, history, and institutional development" are matters that historians normally and regularly take up, and hence that "the worship, piety, practice, and teaching of the various traditions" are matters that they normally and regularly neglect. Perhaps — and this is the possibility that most immediately occurs to me — this contrast is meant to lodge a protest against neglect of matters that concern the day-to-day lives of ordinary believers, that is to say, against too exclusive a concentration on the preoccupations of those who have enjoyed places of prominence and leadership in the public life of the churches. An *ecumenical* church history, it may be thought, must include all aspects of the life of Christian communities. If this is the point of the protest, however, there is no reason why it cannot be made more explicit.

The question has to be raised, of course, whether such a protest is justified. In the case of standard textbooks, which concentrate perforce on public "events" and actions that arguably represent turning points of some sort, it may well be justified. The ordinary life of believers can scarcely be portrayed save by way of "thick description" — a technique to which textbooks, even bulky ones, are ill adapted, and for which they can only substitute generalities and generalizations that are inevitably, from some points of view, misleading. Furthermore, the rhythms of the life of faith within Christian communities do not normally or necessarily correspond to those of the churches' "public" business. Their continuities and discontinuities, whether diachronic or synchronic, are marked on, or constitute, a different grid. It may well be for this reason that studies of, say, liturgical history, which are by no means an endangered species, tend to be carried out independently of ordinary "church history" and, in turn, to be ignored by most teachers who profess the latter discipline. It is easy, as well as correct, to say that this is a shame; but it is not so easy to find ways of integrating these distinct foci into a vision that is genuinely binocular.

Is Principle 5 asserting that what I have called "the ordinary life of believers" is related to "doctrine, history, and institutional development" as their *context?* This is a plausible enough assumption, to be sure: that actions and decisions taken at the level of the churches' public discourse should in fact be rooted in its day-to-day life and activities. It is not always clear, however, that this is the case. Historians of the English Reformation, for example, have long recognized that the context of the Henrician and Edwardian "reforms" was only secondarily the ordinary religious life of ordinary subjects of the English crown. One might even speculate that their immediate context was the life of the royal court, and that the English Reformation is a notable example of a situation in which the generative context of change must be sought in the interests and ideologies that prevailed among public persons. Desirable though it may be to connect "worship, piety, practice, and teaching" with "doctrine, history, and institutional development," which of these constitutes an explanatory or interpretative "context" for the other depends upon contingent circumstance.

6. An ecumenical history of Christianity makes significant use of such sources as iconography, liturgy and worship, oral tradition, tracts and other popular literature, and the archeological record.

This principle is unexceptionable, it seems to me, so long as it is not interpreted to mean that the matters to which sources of this sort provide access have an exclusive claim to the label "contextual." If "context" is taken to mean something like the set of circumstances or conditions that render a particular sequence of change intelligible or that provide the background against which the historian "reads" her sources, then the denotation of "context" is bound to change with the subject of historical inquiry. The prevalence of a certain theme in the popular literature of a past era may well constitute a contextual datum that helps to explain a particular turn in a community's doctrinal formulations; but if one's interest is in that theme itself and the reasons for its popularity, then a converse relationship may obtain: that is, the doctrinal formulations may serve as a factor in the "context" of the literary development. What constitutes context in any specific inquiry is relative to the focus of historical interest. Hence Principle 6 is best read, not as a comment about context, but as an exhortation to historians to cultivate an "ecumenical" spirit in the matter of the types of evidence they consult.

III.

7. An ecumenical history of Christianity acknowledges that each generation and tradition reads the past in the light of its own lively issues.

8. An ecumenical history of Christianity assists in the discovery of parallels in other times and places to contemporary concerns and reexamines divisive issues.

These two principles are introduced under the heading "Commonality." The "commonality" or *koinonia* in question is plainly meant to refer to the "lively issues" and "concerns" that are shared by, and hence common to, historians and readers of history in any particular generation. In short, Principles 7 and 8 want to assert that each generation tends to have a shared agenda that it brings to its study of the past. Within limits, this is undoubtedly true. It needs, however, to be added that the limits in question are not unimportant. Third World historians, for example, may have a different common agenda than their First World colleagues; and there are always mavericks who think that the going agenda is either unprofitable or obtuse.

What is just as interesting, though, and more interesting to me, is the somewhat different "commonality" or *koinonia* these two principles presuppose: that which obtains between the present-day student of past events and eras and the "mentality" or "mind" that guided the thoughts and actions of a particular past. The two principles assert, in effect, that the past is intelligible; and they do so on the ground that communication between the two is possible — even though, since the past cannot talk back, the only active participant in this process of communication is the historian, who is firmly located in her regular position of the latest thing. This one-sided character of the conversation between present and past is *admitted* in Principle 7 and *exploited* in Principle 8.

This is not an appropriate place to raise the question whether it is reasonable to presuppose the "commonality," or communication between present and past, that these two principles assume. It can of course be argued that the historian is not so much "communicating" with the past as constructing it: that texts recounting or portraying the past are little more than elegant works of fiction, shaped by the reworking of a passive matter (called "evidence") that is susceptible of being molded to almost any form. On this demiurgic view of the historian's work, however, it would be difficult to understand why historians argue with one another about what they take to be matters of fact[2] — or, indeed, why anyone would set about the business of writing history (or biography) in the first place.

Even if one wants to set this deliciously skeptical possibility aside, though, the fact that historians read "the past in the light of [their] own lively issues" and are forever searching out "parallels in other times and places to contemporary concerns" might, in the eyes of a critical reader of their works, stimulate at least the ghost of a suspicion about their activities. If it is the business of historians to establish a real communication with the past, even a tentative and perhaps superficial communication, one would expect to see evidence in their writings that the past does not always respond amiably when the "lively issues" of the present dominate the conversation. One would expect, in short, to find that the past has "lively issues" of its own, which might be quite different from the concerns of the his-

---

2. It is interesting in this connection to weigh the current dispute between those who deny that the Holocaust took place and those who repudiate this position as a fiction contrived by (conscious) prejudice. Is this a debate about the realities of the past or merely a conflict between parties who have different interests with regard to a "lively issue" of the present?

torian eager to evoke a sympathetic response to his problems from some ancient pen pal. It is not until the past shrugs its shoulders with indifference that one can be reasonably sure that communication is actually taking place.

It seems, therefore, that the assumption of a "commonality" as between present and past need not — and indeed ought not — be understood simply and solely as an assertion of the past's complaisance when confronted with the needs, interests, and obsessions of a representative "modern." Likeness entails difference, as Plato suggested; and communication can take the form of argument just as frequently as it does that of agreement. The test of the good historian, therefore, may be a willingness to relinquish the demiurgic role — that is, the somewhat imperialistic demand that the past conform to the present — and to allow the past to be different when it seems to offer resistance to the historian's introduction of her own "lively issues" or to exhibit distaste for being clothed in the habiliments of the historian's present. This is not to say that there are no "parallels," only that one must be skeptical when they seem to emerge — as they often do — with unusual and gratifying frequency. Part of the task of the historian *qua* historian is so to *distance* the past as to provide it with a voice that it can employ to shout the historian down: that, indeed, follows from any reasonable understanding of the principle of "context" discussed above. Hence, I judge, one needs to be cautious in supposing that "ecumenicity" or "globality" implies an incorporation of the past in the cosmos of the present.

IV.

9. An ecumenical history of Christianity assists groups of Christians to define their own voices within the conversations among communities of faith and to issue their special challenge to these communities.

10. An ecumenical history of Christianity opens each particular tradition to critical analysis by others.

11. An ecumenical history of Christianity welcomes people to investigate with the historian the Christian past in a spirit of hospitality.

12. An ecumenical history of Christianity approaches its task in the spirit of repentance and forgiveness, avoiding defensiveness with regard to either social location or particular theological, methodological, or ecclesial traditions.

These four principles are introduced under the rubric of "Particularity," perhaps with the intention of contrasting the concerns proper to specific groups of Christians in the present with the "common" concerns that are proper to the entire present generation. What they ask is essentially — again — a moral attitude. The historian is to write in a spirit of fairness — a spirit that evokes the character of each stream of Christian tradition with respect for its strengths and with frankness regarding the contingencies and limitations that are correlative with those strengths.

Two matters here, it seems to me, call for reflection. These principles recognize, on the one hand, that one of the motives that regularly inspire historical inquiry is the desire to identify — and identify with — one's roots. The study of history, in other words, is always, in some degree, the effort to construct, to explore, and to justify a tradition; and the past, therefore, is inevitably construed as precedent. On the other hand, critical history emerged in the modern era precisely as the antidote to tradition, or at any rate to traditionalism; and its not infrequent, and often deliberate, effect has been to deprive people of any sense of rootedness — or (to phrase the matter in a way more consonant with the ideals of the Enlightenment) to set them free from a past construed as precedent.

These two impulses, contrary though they may seem, cohabit in all modern historical inquiry. Traditionalists practice criticism, and antitraditionalists chase after pedigrees down the lengthening corridors of the past. And curiously enough, there is reason in this apparent paradox, for in both cases the past is seen essentially as corresponding to the present: that is to say, as providing case studies in which the dramas of the present are, as it were, preliminarily rehearsed. It is this attitude, I think, that underlies the way in which the principles we are considering deploy the demand for fairness. They advise what might be called "even-handed empathy," which allows room for both traditionalism and criticism in the interest of contemporary ecumenical dialogue.

I am as interested in contemporary ecumenical dialogue as any-one; but I wonder sometimes whether this (eminently orthodox) approach to the matter answers to the true logic of historical investigation. I have already intimated that it is possible to envisage the historian's task as that of conducting a dialogue with the past and that the essence of the historical task thus understood is to provide the past with the opportunity to speak in its own voice. "Critical" history seems to be mostly in the business of conducting autopsies, and "traditionalist" history, in that of painting memorable portraits. It would be interesting, though, if the historian conceived it as his task occasionally to reverse the flow of discourse: to allow the past to challenge — critique? — the present, or at least to squint at it with distaste. The profit of the past may sometimes lie more in what it implicitly says about us than in what we feel constrained to say about it. One is, of course, under no obligation to agree with its deliverances; but it is always useful, as the adage says, to "see ourselves as others see us" — and what more thoroughgoing "other" is there than the past? In such dialogue, which the historian must tentatively and cautiously construct, both the relevance that traditionalism seeks and the distance that criticism presupposes are present — but in a new mode; and fairness is reconceived as fairness to the past itself, rather than primarily to the interests, "lively issues," and identity searches of the present.

V.

13. An ecumenical history of Christianity seeks to understand and clearly to acknowledge its own presuppositions and seeks to overcome its prejudices.

14. An ecumenical history of Christianity acknowledges that no historical account can claim complete objectivity, but seeks fair-minded empathy with the particular stories that comprise the ecumenical history of the Christian people.

With this final pair of principles, we have come back to our starting point and to a recurrent theme of these canons for "ecumenical history": the basically moral exigency of fairness, now construed as a purificatory process involving confession ("clearly to acknowledge its own presuppositions") and restitution ("empathy with the particular stories"). It needs to be noted, however, that the passions of which the historian's soul is thus to be purified are the very impulses that most often drive people to investigate the past.[3] Prejudice and pre-supposition look instinctively to the past for their justification; and history — not excluding critical history — is most often written, one suspects, as part of such a project of reassurance. Their dissolution or correction, therefore, is not likely to be accomplished prior to an engagement with the past. It is when the relics of the past politely decline to conform to a given set of presuppositions and prejudices, or squirm uncomfortably in their Procrustean bed, that the process of purification begins; and what that process requires on the historian's part is a modicum of good sense, a normal endowment of intellectual honesty, and a great deal of courage to face a now unfamiliar and perhaps even threatening past.

Fairness, then, in historians — and this, I suppose, is the point to which I have been coming — has to do in the first instance not with one's attitude toward other contemporary sets of presuppositions and prejudices but precisely with one's attitude toward the past itself. Does the historian ascribe to the past whose relics she studies a subjectivity of its own? Or is the past treated as mere matter for the historian's formation? In the former case, the historian enters into what I have called dialogue with the past, and never stops learning new things; in the latter case the historian constructs the past, whether as a weapon for use in contemporary debate or as a pleasing work of art. In my estimation, what one *ought* to mean by "ecumenical" or "inclusive" history is the former: a history that lets the past itself into a conversation, on the understanding that it may, from time to time, practice criticism itself. And of course that means any past one may happen to be dealing with. How a one-volume textbook, if written along these lines, might look or fare, I cannot say; but it would be interesting to make the effort to find out.

---

3. One must not of course discount curiosity, the driving instinct of the gossip.

3. *The Global Context of Ecumenical History*

Günther Gassmann

1. The Principles and One Addition

The statements and their explication in "Christian History in Ecumenical Perspective: Principles of Historiography" are most helpful. They could, indeed, serve as stimulating and sensitizing guidelines for all who, in one form or another, are engaged in writing church history on whatever level and in whatever specific perspective. The principles could be used as "signposts" that would assist in avoiding all limited and narrow perspectives in historiography, which are, to a certain degree, unavoidable because of the specific context, formation, and subjectivity of those who are writing church history. But even where these principles are observed, the result will not be a "complete objectivity," as the last principle confirms. Indeed, the times of historicism have long gone by. Now the most fascinating accounts of church history clearly carry the mark of the author's personal interpretation and are often challenging in their one-sidedness and provocative in their critical judgments.

This last point leads me to the observation that the principles could have included an additional one: An ecumenical history of Christianity is *critical* in the sense of exposing the failures and sins in Christian history when this history is judged in the light of the God-given mission of the church, revealed in Jesus Christ, sustained

37

by the Holy Spirit, and oriented toward the fulfillment of the reign
of God.

2. Is All Christian History Ecumenical History?

I have one real problem with the principles, and that concerns the
terminology used. The following terms occur: "Christian history in
ecumenical perspective," "ecumenical history of Christianity," "ecumenical church history," "church history in an ecumenical perspective." They seem to be applied interchangeably. I am not worried by
the two terms "church history" and "history of Christianity" (even
though one could reflect here on certain distinctions, e.g., in the way
in which Trutz Rendtorff uses the expression *Christentumsgeschichte*
— in distinction to church history — to indicate the explicit or implicit
influence of Christianity on the cultural and social fabric of societies).
I am rather concerned by the use of the term *ecumenical*. It is used,
as far as I can see, sometimes in the specific sense of the diverse efforts
toward Christian unity, including common mission and service, and
more often in a rather broad, unspecific way in the sense of global,
comprehensive, all-inclusive, and the like. There is, of course, no
"official" definition of *ecumenical*. And the great ecumenist Willem
Visser 't Hooft has identified seven possible meanings of the term,
reaching from "pertaining to or representing the whole (inhabited)
world" to "that quality or attitude which expresses the consciousness
of and desire for Christian Unity." He believes that the new usage of
the term in the sense of "that which concerns the unity and world-wide
mission of the Church of Jesus Christ" seems to have established itself
with a good prospect of permanence.[1] In a similar way the Central
Committee of the WCC already in 1951 accepted the following reference to *ecumenical:*

> It is important to insist that this word (i.e. ecumenical), which comes
> from the Greek word for the whole inhabited earth, is properly used
> to describe everything that relates to the whole task of the whole

1. Willem Adolf Visser 't Hooft, "The Word 'Ecumenical' — Its History
and Use," in Ruth Rouse and Stephen Charles Neill, eds., *A History of the
Ecumenical Movement 1517-1948,* 3rd ed. (Geneva: WCC, 1986), 735-40.

Church to bring the Gospel to the whole world. It therefore covers equally the missionary movement and the movement toward unity.[2]

Even the attempts in the seventies to extend the dimension of *ecumenical* by relating the concern for the unity of the church to the unity (or renewal) of humankind have not basically changed the earlier definition. Such a change can be observed today when some ecumenists subsume the dialogue and relationships with other religions under the term *ecumenical*. But I prefer to stick with the ecumenical tradition of conceiving *ecumenical* in a narrower sense.

It is on the basis of this presupposition that I want to respond to the question in the heading of this section: "Is all Christian history ecumenical history?" Asked in the framework of the more narrow definition of *ecumenical,* this question provides us, I believe, exactly with one criterion for a critical presentation of Christian or church history, the need of which was underlined above. A first, very general answer to the question would then be that by far not all Christian history has been and is ecumenical history. Much of Christian history is marked by division, separation, and strife, a refusal — whether explicit or unavoidable — to be faithful to God's gift and calling to be visibly and effectively the one People of God, the one Body of Christ, the one Temple of the Holy Spirit, grounded in the one baptism, nourished by sharing together the one gospel in word and sacrament, lived out in common witness and service among all people. It is precisely because of this history of division and unfaithfulness — which is, of course, much more complex than indicated here — that an "ecumenical history," a counterhistory, was necessary as an attempt to return to faithfulness to God's purpose in the history of the church. And with this qualification we may take up the question again and modify the earlier response by saying, "Christian history is also marked by and embraces within itself ecumenical history."

2. Lukas Vischer, ed., *A Documentary History of the Faith and Order Movement 1927-1963* (St. Louis: Bethany Press, 1963), 178.

3. What, Then, Is Ecumenical History?

The appreciation of the principles and the questioning of one particular aspect related to them was a necessary "prolegomenon" for dealing with the assigned topic, "The Global Context of Ecumenical History." In the framework of the rather unspecified use of *ecumenical* in the principles, this heading had for me the character of a tautology. If *ecumenical* is identified with *global,* this is obvious. But when *ecumenical* is used in a more specific way, then *global* becomes again a criterion for a critical presentation of ecumenical history: "Is all ecumenical history global?" And this is the direction I would like to follow.

Let us, first, try to define the terms somewhat more clearly. On the basis of what has been indicated above I tend to understand *ecumenical history* in the sense of those efforts and movements within Christian or church history whose aim was and is to overcome divisions among Christians and churches and to bring them to forms of communion that will enable them to confess together the one apostolic faith, mutually to recognize and share in their sacraments and ministries, to live with each other in spiritual communion of common prayer and worship and in solidarity of sharing in each other's joys and suffering, to proclaim together in the whole world the gospel of God's grace and love in Jesus Christ, to serve all people in need, and to become in all this an instrument of God's saving and renewing purpose for all humanity and creation. There are different ways of expressing these marks and goals of ecumenical history.[3]

4. What Is the "Global Context" of Ecumenical History?

The term *global context* in the heading I tend to understand, first of all, in the critical sense indicated above. Not all ecumenical history has been, in fact, global. But *global* is, indeed, according to the more

---

3. Cf., e.g., the Statement of the WCC Assembly on "The Unity of the Church as Koinonia: Gift and Calling," in Michael Kinnamon, ed., *Signs of the Spirit: Official Report of the Seventh Assembly, Canberra, Australia, 7-20 February 1991* (Geneva: WCC and Grand Rapids: Eerdmans, 1991), 172-74.

specific definitions of *ecumenical,* or, theologically speaking, according to the purpose of God for all humanity and creation, a fundamental dimension of ecumenical history. It is, however, an imperative, a task grounded in the indicative of God's gift and offer of communion and new life for all, and not simply and always a historical reality. In addition, *global context* in relation to ecumenical history refers in my opinion to more than the worldwide dimension of this history; instead, it refers to the "whole Christian Church on earth" according to Martin Luther's Small Catechism. I understand *global context* also in the sense of *world history* as the wider context in which ecumenical history (as well as Christian or church history) has its place and to which it is related in manifold interdependence.

In conclusion: a paraphrase of the heading for this chapter could be "The Worldwide and World-Historical Context of Ecumenical Efforts and Movements within Christian History." This indicates, indeed, an essential perspective both for our conception of ecumenical history, in the more specific sense defined above, and for the writing of Christian history in its ecumenical dimension. Thus, we have to take into account three levels: (1) ecumenical history as it has actually happened and is happening — the object of the writing of Christian history, which, however, cannot claim to grasp and present this history in full objectivity, but should be guided by principles like the ones proposed in this book; (2) the history of (ecumenical) ideas as an integral part of ecumenical history (ecumenism) — the prescriptive theories, concepts, ideals, and goals that are intended to shape ecumenical history and that, with their historical realizations and failures, provide the writing of Christian history with intrinsic criteria for positive and critical evaluation; (3) the writing of Christian history itself, with its task to describe, analyze, and evaluate this complex mix of ideas and historical reality.

With the help of the principles and these additional reflections and (it is hoped) clarifications, I would now like to draw out some lines in application of what has been said so far.

5. The Global Claim of Ecumenical History

Christian history has included from its early Christian beginnings the element of ecumenical history in the sense of the continuing struggle to preserve or to restore the unity of the church. At certain times this was even the dominating force in shaping church history. From the beginning this ecumenical history was also accompanied by the claim to be *global* in perspective. *Global* was understood both in the sense of the known world at a given time and in the sense of penetrating and shaping world history within the given geographical boundaries of the "Christian world." This global claim received a new quality in modern time *(Neuzeit),* when the world in its full extension became known, together with the recognition that this world was by far not identical with the "Christian world" conceived from a European and Mediterranean center (with some extensions beyond). This new situation led to the missionary expansion, especially in the nineteenth century, with its global claims ("The Evangelization of the World in this Generation"), and, partly as a consequence of this expansion (and of European emigration to the "New World" in North and South America), to the emergence of the modern ecumenical movement.

This movement, the most significant expression of ecumenical history in the course of Christian history, again began with the claim of being global in perspective. It was especially the new experience of a smaller, interdependent world at the end of the nineteenth and the beginning of the twentieth centuries that made the claim to globality one of the dominant orientations of the modern ecumenical movement since the first great World Missionary Conference at Edinburgh in 1910. The inspiring figure of this conference, John R. Mott, declared at its close that "gathered together from different nations and races and communions," the delegates had come to realize their oneness in Christ.[4] The movements for Life and Work, for Faith and Order, and the International Missionary Council in the first half of the twentieth century were characterized by the same "global ethos" in their intention to be worldwide and consciously oriented also toward world history by seeking to render a service to peace among the nations, to help resist the emerging totalitarian ideologies and systems in Europe, to assist in creating more just and humane conditions for large parts of the world's population. Even the pioneers of the Faith and Order movement, focusing on overcoming the divisive doctrinal differences between the churches, understood this task as a precondition and

4. Cf. Rouse and Neill, 361.

contribution to common Christian witness and service in the whole world, as a complement to the "secular ecumenism" represented since 1919 by the League of Nations.

Yes, the *Geistesgeschichte,* the history of ideas, of ecumenical history has been global in orientation — global in the double meaning indicated above. But at the same time ecumenical history, especially in the late nineteenth century and the twentieth century, has been emphatically local in its perspectives. "Local ecumenism" in the framework of a nation, a part of a nation, a city, has been the focus for many ecumenical efforts. The place or context where Christians actually live together, or rather live side by side in separation, conflict, or at best coexistence, is the context where ecumenism has to begin, where ecumenical history is "earthed." This claim to be local must not contradict the other claim to be global. The local focus can be justified in its own right. It is rather the interrelation between these two dimensions that is the problem and that has occupied recent ecumenical reflection more than ever before. Thus, it is important to note that on the level of ecumenical theory (we will look at the praxis in a moment) these two claims have found equal attention whereby the focus on local, like the one on global, is not limited to the given Christian constituency but is often oriented toward the wider social and cultural situation in which Christians may even constitute a minority. Thus, the global context in the theories of ecumenical history is accompanied by the local context of this history; and the way in which this duality has been coped with in ecumenical theory and history is one important element for the writing of Christian history.

6. The Global Failures of Ecumenical History

Parallel to the claim to globality in ecumenical history one must now point to the failures and distortions of this claim in the course of history. Only a few indications must suffice again. The worldwide orientation of Christian history and the stream of ecumenical history within it were up to the modern time obviously limited geographically, and even conceived as radiating out from certain centers like Constantinople and Rome. The realization of the worldwide orientation was often achieved with the help of secular powers; the recent five-hundredth anniversary of the European discovery of South America was a reminder of only one particular instance in which this has happened and of how this has made ecumenical relations so difficult. These same developments in Christian history have also determined the way in which globality — in the sense of the relation of Christian history to world history — has been realized. In many cases Christian and world history have come in the "Constantinian era" to be nearly identical or intertwined in ways that were, to say the least, highly ambivalent. This general impression of the first fifteen hundred years of Christian history is overwhelming, but it is not the full picture. Here, the principles could certainly help to rediscover all those movements and persons in Christian history that struggled, within the limitations of their ideas and contexts, to be faithful to the claims to globality.

Also in modern times the global context was often conceived and realized in a manner that in the analysis of later generations was again marked by limitations and distortions. The missionary movement comes immediately to mind, with the outreach of European and North American Christianity having emphatically global orientation and at the same time remaining bound to the missionary home bases and exporting cultural and social forms and values that were imposed on indigenous forms and values. The ecumenical element in the earlier missionary movement was primarily one of allocating specific areas for missionary work to the different missionary societies (the principle of "comity"). Again, in all this committed and sacrificial work one dare not ignore the exceptions, the attempts of individuals truly to think and act globally in respect to those to whom they were sent with the gospel. But in the historian's analysis, the failures to be global in the way the missionary outreach was understood and realized are the prevailing conclusion. Even the already mentioned World Missionary Conference, which marks the beginning of the movement toward true globality, was predominantly an Anglo-Saxon event and far from representing worldwide Christianity at that time.

This "North Atlantic" orientation was also present in the participants and outlook of the other ecumenical efforts in the first half of the twentieth century and was, in a way, a contradiction of their global claims. That this was also true for the Rome-centered and explicitly nonecumenical position of the Roman Catholic Church has been obvious and became increasingly a point of internal Catholic criticism in the years before the Second Vatican Council. The focus on local ecumenism in the second half of the nineteenth century in North America and then later in Europe, especially in England, led to national structures, associations, and conversations. This was an important development in itself, but with few exceptions the local emphasis was not consciously related to a global perspective. However, in these earlier stages of modern ecumenical history, seen and judged from our present position, there were also the beginnings of a renewal that was aiming to see and implement the global context of ecumenical history in ways that were believed to be more in conformity with God's purpose for the worldwide mission of the church.

7. Resolving the Contradiction between Claims and Failures?

In section five I referred to the claims to globality in ecumenical history up to the first stages of the modern ecumenical movement, and in section six I indicated the failures and distortions on the historical realization of these claims. A temptation would be to demonstrate now, in a Hegelian fashion, the overcoming of this contradiction between claims and realizations in the form of a qualitative new, theologically more adequate perception and implementation of globality in present ecumenical history (since about 1948). This would be, however, far too simplistic a schema, which would force ecumenical history and the writing of this history into a preconceived pattern and would negate the complexity that is a characteristic of all history. This schema would be too simplistic because the claims to globality, the "thesis," would be in themselves conditioned by the unavoidably limited perceptions of the world based on a thoroughgoing Eurocentrism up to the present time. (This Eurocentrism, was, of course, the result of the close interrelation between secular/political and church history; consider for example the creation of terms like "Near East" or "Far East" from a center located in London.) These claims were also limited by the concepts of a "symphony," a harmonious interpenetration of church history and world history in terms of a Christian world, society, and culture.

The "anti-thesis," on the other hand, the failures and distortions of the claims to globality as judged from our present understanding of the global mission of the church, are therefore in many ways not only a conscious refusal to be consistent with the global claims but also a historical consequence of the ways in which these claims have been understood. But in the midst of these limitations, as has been already mentioned, we find also individuals, groups, and movements that have struggled to transcend, with their ideas and actions, a Euro-centric view of the world as the field for Christian mission "overseas," who have conceived of the relationship of ecumenical history to world history not in terms of domination and cultural colonialism but in terms of "salt" and "leaven," of service to the manifold needs of humanity in faithfulness to God's saving and renewing will. In many instances these faithful efforts, in the contexts of their times, were so closely intermingled with the failures and distortions — the missionary and ecumenical movements provide again innumerable examples for this — that all generalizing judgments, all neat compartmentalizing attributions of positive or negative developments, would fail adequately to circumscribe historical reality.

This poses a certain dilemma for the writing of Christian history because some form of generalization will be necessary if one does not want to be "drowned" in the oscillating waters of endless differentiations when trying to capture and describe complex realities. In the majority of cases of historical research and writing this dilemma can be overcome, at best, by discerning prevailing features and tendencies within a complex reality — and that was the intention in sections five and six.

8. The Global Context in Present Ecumenical History

In the light of the preceding considerations it cannot be the purpose of this section to point out how we have reached a new stage of clarity that leaves past complexities behind. Rather, it is my conviction that the prevailing tendencies and features during recent decades of this ecumenical era are the many attempts to discover a new vision of globality in accordance with the God-given mission of the church and to translate this vision into historical reality. That this is not a completely new development but stands in a certain continuity with earlier, pioneering attempts in the late nineteenth and earlier twentieth centuries can be shown and belongs to the differentiated picture of claims, failures, and realizations referred to above. But this same continuity comprehends within itself also in our time examples of failures and distortions in relation to the prevailing tendencies and features.

I would like to refer to a few examples that demonstrate the new vision of globality in present ecumenical history, together with developments that led to this new vision.

The World Council of Churches (WCC) after its foundation in 1948 was conceived as a fellowship of churches whose representation in the WCC and its governing bodies should reflect both their confessional and their geographical distribution. This compromise between the advocates of a confessional and of a geographical principle of representation was clearly intended to underline the global, worldwide character of this new fellowship. The first section of the 1948 Amsterdam Assembly on the "The Universal Church in God's Design" sounded a leitmotiv that was to be developed in theological reflection and practical application in the history of the WCC. The overall theme of Amsterdam, "Man's Disorder and God's Design," taken up in two sections on "The Church and the Disorder of Society" and "The Church and the International Disorder," announced the other dimension of the global context, namely that the worldwide fellowship of the WCC perceived itself in an active relationship to world history. The Commission of the Churches on International Affairs, already constituted before the foundation of the WCC, was one of the structural expressions of this orientation, together with the work in "Church and Society" and many programs and projects.

The 1968 Uppsala Assembly of the WCC marks a most significant step in developing the global vision and reality of the WCC. The WCC, up to Uppsala still dominated by Europeans and North Americans, was challenged by a vision of God's universal history presently realized in the new revolutionary movements toward national independence, racial and economic justice, and liberation from oppressive, dehumanizing forces in all parts of the world, especially in the South. Its slightly less optimistic theological formulation found this vision in the section on "The Holy Spirit and the Catholicity of the Church." The section report said, "The purpose of Christ is to bring people of all times, of all races, of all places, of all conditions, into an organic and living unity in Christ by the Holy Spirit under the universal fatherhood of God"; the report saw the goal of the work for Christian unity in a "genuinely universal council" that could speak for all Christians. One of the key sentences of this report, "The Church is bold in speaking of itself as the sign of the coming unity of mankind,"[5] provided the orientation for the study of the Faith and Order Commission on "The Unity of the Church and the Unity of Humankind" (1969-74), which was then resumed under the less controversial title "The Unity of the Church and the Renewal of Human Community" (1982-90).

The conciliar perspective of Christian unity, indicated at Uppsala, found a fuller expression, prepared by studies of Faith and Order, in the statement on unity of the 1975 Assembly at Nairobi with its much quoted formula of a "conciliar fellowship of local churches which are themselves truly united."[6] The statement thus continued the focus on local unity of the famous 1961 New Delhi statement on unity, and integrated it with the universal expression and significance of Christian unity that emerged so strongly at Uppsala. This integration of the local and global perspectives in their interdependence was theologically undergirded in the work of Faith and Order, whose now famous "Baptism, Eucharist and Ministry" document, to quote only one example, states, "Eucharistic celebrations have to do with the whole Church, and the whole Church is involved in each local eucharistic celebration."[7]

The global perspective of ecumenical history was clearly present also in the program, issues, and participants of the last two Assemblies, at Vancouver in 1983 and Canberra in 1991. This perspective was increasingly broadened by including also the concerns of the care for creation. The statement on "The Unity of the Church as Koinonia — Gift and Calling" of the Canberra Assembly states the purpose of common mission as "witnessing to the Gospel of God's grace to all people and serving the whole of creation." It relates, like Nairobi, the

5. Norman Goodall, ed., *The Uppsala Report 1968* (Geneva: WCC, 1968), 17.

6. David M. Paton, ed., *Breaking Barriers: Nairobi 1975* (London: SPCK and Grand Rapids: Eerdmans, 1975), 60.

7. *Baptism, Eucharist and Ministry: Eucharist,* para. 19.

local and global perspectives by pointing out that the communion (koinonia) among the churches "will be expressed on the local and universal levels through conciliar forms of life and action."[8]

The WCC has thus become the forum where Christianity (or larger parts of it) has become truly worldwide in character and at the same time finds itself indissolubly bound up with a threatened creation and the destiny of an interdependent world and its ambivalences, possibilities, and struggles for survival. This is the new "world theater" of ecumenical history, where churches have rediscovered the universality of the church. This reality is experienced in their manifold contacts and relationships across all continents; exchange of spiritual and theological insights; sharing of resources; solidarity with churches in need; glimpses of the diverse social, political, and cultural situations in which churches live and by which they are shaped in their thinking and life. And there is the experience of the involvement of Christians and churches in the social and political struggles of our time, for example in the world-historical changes in Eastern Europe. All this has made the global perspective and the catholic dimension of ecumenical history an experienced reality. Developments in Christian World Communions, including the Roman Catholic Church, have played an important role in this strengthening and broadening of the global perspective of ecumenical history. Confessional organizations like the World Alliance of Reformed Churches or the Baptist World Alliance, but also the Lambeth Conferences of all Anglican Bishops, were since the late nineteenth century among the first structures that enabled an experience of the global reality of the church. In their further development in this century these World Communions have become increasingly a true expression of their original goals by giving member churches from all continents a full share in their life and work. This effort toward globality in the sense of an equal, inclusive, and sharing partnership of all members has found its expression in the concept of a "communion of churches," first conceived in the Anglican Communion, which during the last decade has also shaped the understanding of a "Lutheran Communion" or "Communion of Lutheran Churches" in the Lutheran World Federation and which is now becoming a general ecumenical concept. In addition to the Christian

8. Kinnamon, 172-74.

World Communions, voluntary ecumenical organizations like the Student Christian Movement, the United Bible Societies, and others have already for a long time contributed to a growing awareness and experience of the global dimension of ecumenical history.

A most significant change in the understanding and realization of the worldwide character of the church was initiated by the Second Vatican Council. In contrast to the preconciliar ecclesiology and structure, which was centered on Rome and conceived in a static institutional and uniformistic mode, the new ecclesiology decreed at the Council was clearly oriented to the universal nature of the church, a worldwide communion in catholic diversity, sent to all the nations as instrument (sacrament) of God's uniting and saving purpose. This global dimension in its twofold meaning, referring to the universal nature of the church and to the mission of this church within the family of nations and their world history, is announced already in the first sentences of *Lumen Gentium* and then developed in all texts of the Council. It is grounded and explicated in the framework of a vision of salvation history that includes all reality in the perspective of its final fulfillment. Also in the relationship between the local and global nature of the church, the Council transcended the former preeminence of the universal concept of the church centered in Rome by rehabilitating, with the help of a eucharistic ecclesiology, the ecclesial reality of the local churches in whom the church of Jesus Christ is fully present. The local or particular churches are no longer seen as subordinate and only partial expressions of the universal church, but "it is in them and formed out of them that the one and unique Catholic Church exists."[9] This rehabilitation of the local church has as one of its consequences that these churches must be "incarnated," rooted in the diverse societies and cultures,[10] and thus manifest in their diversity the true catholicity of the church. This new vision of the global, that is, universal and catholic, nature of the church is of great importance far beyond the Roman Catholic Church, because it is presented in the form of a comprehensive theological discourse that no other Christian World Communion or the WCC has been able to develop. The historical implementation of this vision can be seen in many parts of the Roman

9. *Lumen Gentium,* 23.
10. *Ad Gentes,* 10, 15, 19-22.

Catholic Church, but it is an implementation that has led at the same time to internal tensions and anxieties and even to attempts to return to a preconciliar *"Romanitas."*

These last remarks bring us back to the complex mixture of visions (or claims) and their limited historical realization or even distortion. This could be also shown in relation to the other attempts within the fellowship of the WCC or in Christian World Communions, where we observe many examples of a continuing or new provincial-ism, a captivity to ethnic or nationalistic loyalties, a new particularism in the form of interest groups and caucuses, and thus a nonreception of the global visions and perspectives formulated at ecumenical meet-ings. Thus, our present ecumenical history reveals remarkable concepts and implementations of its global perspective as one of its outstanding features, but not without the *"simul"* of faithful achievement and all too human failure.

9. Conclusions for the Writing of Christian History

There is no point in providing a summary of what has been said in the preceding eight sections of this chapter. Too much of it was already, given the breadth of the topic, in the form of summaries of theological concepts and historical realizations. What has become clear for me in relation to the task of writing Christian history can now be indicated in a few sentences.

First, the global perspective of Christian history is fundamental to this history and has become a dominating mark in present ecumeni-cal history. Any writing of Christian history that does not take this perspective into account would betray its subject.

Second, the development of this global perspective in the history of theology and in the history of Christianity must be seen as a dynamic and complex process. The interplay between ideas and reality, past efforts and present critical judgments on them, traces of new visions and their later working out, efforts to be faithful to God's universal purpose and the often only partial realization of these efforts or their negation — this interplay is the stuff that could make writing on the global perspectives of ecumenical history a fascinating enterprise.

Third, if the term *global perspective* would be interpreted with the help of the term *catholic* — and glimpses of this have been given in this chapter, though I have tried to stay as much as possible with the term *global* — then both the theological and the comprehensive dimensions of the global perspective of ecumenical history would be strengthened. *Catholic* is here understood in the sense of the "whole Christian church on earth," with its constitutive diversity of the expressions of Christian faith and life, in diverse contexts and traditions, bound together in faithfulness to the one *apostolic* tradition in time and space, called to a serving *holiness* in an unholy world, challenged to manifest universally and locally the God-given *unity* of the church of Jesus Christ.

The inclusion of this dimension of catholicity would not only provide a theological framework for the application of the principles outlined in chapter 1, but would also serve as an essential theological criterion and open up the broad horizon of God's catholic purpose for writing on the global perspective of ecumenical history.

II. CASE STUDIES: INTERACTING WITH THE PRINCIPLES

4. The Arian Heresy?

Frederick W. Norris

Perhaps one of the more interesting chapters within a conception of ecumenical church history is the modern concern to identify and evaluate the Arians. Arianism has often been viewed as the classical heresy and pictured in those terms.[1] At times its leaders both in the early and in the later phases have been depicted as liberals or progressives who overstepped the limits of tradition, who not only enlisted philosophy in the service of theology but subordinated theology to philosophy and abandoned deep concerns of worship and holy writ. At other times they have been viewed as conservatives who did not adapt to new situations, who depended heavily on older theological positions such as an extreme monotheism and a Christology built upon the work of Clement of Alexandria or Origen. On the most cursory examination of many historical surveys, however, we

1. Joseph Lienhard, "Recent Studies in Arianism," *Religious Studies Review* 8 (1982): 331; "The 'Arian' Controversy: Some Categories Reconsidered," *Theological Studies* 48 (1987): 415-17. In the latter article Lienhard suggests that the name "Arian" is misleading and that theologically the two traditions, which he entitles "miahypostatic" and "dyohypostatic," are more appropriate in categorizing the early "Arian" debate. The first describes the position of Athanasius, Marcellus of Ancyra, and a number of Western theologians; the second includes Eusebius of Caesarea and a number of Eastern theologians as well as Arius. These categories, although technical, emerge from the texts and thus are quite helpful.

The primary and secondary literature about fourth-century Arianism is large. I have chosen to concentrate on the Greek East for primary sources and on the recent debate in English for secondary works.

can see that these characteristics too often owe their creation or emphasis to the "orthodox" victors. They are based on the winners' perceptions of Arianism rather than on the Arians' own self-understanding.[2]

To operate within another approach is difficult although not impossible. Every "Arian" known to us now appears in a truncated corpus, if there is enough material to call it a corpus. We can indicate that Arius wrote the *Thalia,* but we do not have a copy of it, only phrases from it referred to by his opponents. His three extant epistles tell us little about him or his positions.[3] Some homilies from Asterius are extant, but they hardly represent all that he wrote.[4] Indeed many

2. John Henry Newman, *The Arians of the Fourth Century,* revised ed. (London: Longmans, Green & Co., 1891), had set forth that kind of interpretation in great detail. Some of the more recent and often used histories of Christian doctrine, written in English, deal with Arians as conservators of earlier positions much influenced by philosophical schools. See J. N. D. Kelly, *Early Christian Doctrines,* 5th ed. (San Francisco: Harper & Row, 1976), esp. 231 for Arius and 249 for Eunomius. The difference between these views and some of the newer insights is clearly visible in comparing the first and second editions of Justo Gonzalez, *A History of Christian Thought,* vol. 1 (Nashville: Abingdon, 1970), 265-81, and (1987), 261-90, esp. 261-65. Jaroslav Pelikan, *The Christian Tradition: A History of the Development of Doctrine,* vol. 1, *The Emergence of the Catholic Tradition (100-600)* (Chicago: University of Chicago Press, 1971), esp. 195-200, presents a more balanced survey, particularly in noting the Arians' worship and exegetical concerns.

3. See G. C. Stead, "The *Thalia* of Arius and the Testimony of Athanasius," *The Journal of Theological Studies,* n.s. 29 (1978): 20-52; M. L. West, "The Metre of Arius' *Thalia,*" *The Journal of Theological Studies,* n.s. 33 (1982): 98-105. Among others, Rowan Williams, "The Quest for the Historical *Thalia,*" and Stuart Hall, "The *Thalia* of Arius in Athanasius' Accounts," both in *Arianism: Historical and Theological Reassessments: Papers from the Ninth International Conference on Patristic Studies, Oxford, September 5-10, 1983,* Patristic Monograph Series 11 (Cambridge, MA: The Philadelphia Patristic Foundation, 1985), 1-36, 37-58, warn from different perspectives of various problems in getting at Arius and the Arians through these fragments. Gustav Bardy, *Recherches sur St. Lucien d'Antioche et son école* (Paris: Beauchesne, 1936), 216-78, probably offers the most accessible collection of Arius's fragments.

4. Marcel Richard, ed., *Asterii Sophistae Commentariorum in Psalmos,* Symbolae Osloenses Fasc. Supplet. XVI (Oslo: Brogger, 1956). Bardy, 341-54, offers a collection of fragments from Asterius. Wolfram Kinzig, *In Search of Asterius: Studies on the Authorship of the Homilies on the Psalms,* Forschungen zur Kirchen- und Dogmengeschichte 47 (Gottingen: Vandenhoek & Ruprecht, 1990), argues that

leaders who supported positions similar to those of Arius are known
to us only by name, not by any works at all.[5] Representatives of the
later phases do not fare much better. We have Eunomius's *Apology,*
parts of his *Apology for the Apology,* a *Confession of Faith,* and some
other fragments, but we do not have his commentary on Romans.[6]
We must deal with Aetius on the basis of his *Syntagmation,* a com-
pendium of tightly constructed enthymemes that portray logical syl-
logisms or conundrums, and a few fragments. Thus, he looks precisely
like the "logic-chopper" whom the orthodox describe as fundamentally flawed, but we do not know what else he might have written that
would give any other side of his life and thought.[7] Indeed the church
history of Philostorgius, which was written from the Arian point of
view, comes down to us only in the epitome of Photius, who had read
the work and left us extensive notes about its contents.[8] The lack of
materials due to both the accidents of history and designed suppression
has not left Arians voiceless, but their mighty chorus does not sing
their oratorios.[9] During much of Athanasius's career they drowned

these homilies were written by a different Asterius, who flourished between 385 and
410 C.E. Karl-Heinz Uthemann reviewed Kinzig's work in *Vigiliae Christianae* 45
(1991): 194-203, and Kinzig replied in "Asterius Sophista oder Asterius Ignotus?
Eine Antwort," *Vigiliae Christianae* 45 (1991): 388-98. In my judgment the
identification of Richard, which Uthemann defends, still stands.

5. One can find mention of these folks in the ecclesiastical histories of
Socrates and Sozomen, who tended to support what became "orthodox" perspectives, and of Philostorgius, who was himself later an Arian.

6. *Eunomius: The Extant Works,* text and trans. by Richard Paul Vaggione,
Oxford Early Christian Texts (Oxford: Clarendon Press, 1987). This remarkable
volume gives us access to Eunomius in the best possible way: his texts critically
edited and clearly translated.

7. See Lionel Wickham, "The *Syntagmation* of Aetius the Anomean," *The
Journal of Theological Studies,* n.s. 19 (1968): 532-69.

8. Philostorgius, *Kirchengeschichte,* ed. Joseph Bidez, 2nd ed., in *Die grie-
chische christliche Schriftsteller,* Friedhelm Winkelmann, gen. ed. (Berlin: Aka-
demie-Verlag, 1972). There is an English translation of Philostorgius in *The
Ecclesiastical History of Sozomen . . . also The Ecclesiastical History of Philostorgius
as epitomized by Photius,* trans. Edward Walford, Bohn's Ecclesiastical Library
(London: Henry G. Bohn, 1855).

9. Philostorgius *H.E.* 11.5, *GCS,* 135 notes that Eunomius's books were
condemned to be burned. The law appears in the *Theodosian Code* 16.5.34. See
The Theodosian Code and Novels and the Sirmondian Constitutions, trans., comm.,

out his voice. When Gregory Nazianzen arrived in Constantinople during 379 his small group met in a chapel because all the major churches sang Arian songs.

Because so much of the Arian corpus is imbedded within that of orthodox writers, the Arians at times have become ventriloquists' dummies through whom the orthodox have spoken. In his attacks on Arius, Athanasius selectively quotes from Arius's works. He gives parts of an argument, but the key words and some of the inferences reflect his construction of his opponent's views. It is not certain that they always state positions taken by Arius.[10] Later Arians are said to have claimed that they knew as much as God knew about divine nature, but the apparent quotation of their views comes to us in the ecclesiastical history of Socrates with no clear attribution to where one might find it in the works of Eunomius.[11] Given Aetius's bold theological confidence, one might suggest that he could make such a remark, but there is no evidence to demand that the arrogant claim itself was ever written by an Arian leader. Orthodox polemics may be its source. Some lesser mind within Arian circles might have made such a statement, but we have no overwhelming reason to assume that better advocates of Arianism might not themselves have refuted it as going beyond the pale.

When we turn to the teachings of the Arians, one of the striking aspects is how much variation there was within the positions of their leaders during the fourth century, indeed within the period of only a

---

glossary, and bib. by Clyde Pharr with Theresa Sherrer Davidson and Mary Brown Pharr (New York: Greenwood Press, 1952). R. P. C. Hanson, *The Search for the Doctrine of God: The Arian Controversy, 318-381* (Edinburgh: T. & T. Clark, 1988), and Thomas Kopecek, *A History of Neo-Arianism,* Patristic Monograph Series 8 (Cambridge, MA: The Philadelphia Patristic Foundation, 1979), both give the Arians relatively clear voices.

10. Stead, 20-52, and Hall, 27-58, clearly point out these questionable tactics. Charles Kannengiesser, "Current Theology: Arius and the Arians," *Theological Studies* 44 (1983): 459, thinks that in spite of the significant problems, literary critical study can lead us back to Arius through Athanasius.

11. Socrates *H.E.* 4.7, *PG* 67, 473B-C. Vaggione, Fragment ii, 167-70, 178-79, finds this fragment to be genuine. That is fascinating since Vaggione takes great care to give Eunomius his due. Lionel Wickham, 565-66, n. 1, who more often points out the deficiencies of Aetius and Eunomius, thinks that this apparent quotation is an invention of the orthodox.

few decades. Arius in his poetic *Thalia* seems to have developed an
apophatic theology, one that insisted upon the incomprehensibility of
God's nature. He worked conservatively from Alexandrian teaching; a
number of his tenets can be found in writings from Clement of
Alexandria.[12] His argument that we cannot possibly know the full
nature of God since our own nature is such a mystery to us is in fact a
position quite similar to that taken by the Cappadocian fathers (Basil of
Caesarea, Gregory of Nazianzus, and Gregory of Nyssa) against the
so-called Neo-Arians of the mid-fourth century and beyond. Both the
moderate Arians present at the council of Antioch in 341 and the
Neo-Arians of later decades had already rejected Arius's view of God's
incomprehensible nature.[13] Rowan Williams describes the later Arians,
particularly Aetius and Eunomius, as teaching a "curious revelational
positivism." He views "strict Eunomianism, with its single revealed
divine name, *agennetos,* exhaustively expressing God's simplicity, as a
rather disastrously clumsy effort to give this position a measure of
philosophical respectability — robbing it, in the process, of much of its
religious seriousness."[14]

Yet Asterius, an early Arian, well documented as such by the early
church histories, including the Arian historian Philostorgius, is in his
homilies rather difficult to distinguish from Athanasius or the so-called
orthodox.[15] Aloys Grillmeier, the great modern historian of early
Christology, has even suggested that Asterius must have had a change

12. Rudolph Lorenz, *Arius Judaizans? Untersuchungen zur dogmen-geschichtlichen Einordnung des Arius,* Forschungen zur Kirchen- und Dogmengeschichte 31 (Gottingen: Vandenhoek & Ruprecht, 1979), demonstrates that Arius was not a Judaizer as the orthodox charged. He finds a number of Arius's positions similar to those taken by Clement.

13. Athanasius *De synodis* 22, *PG* 26, 719C. Both Aetius and Eunomius claim that the nature of God is knowable, indeed that the name of that nature is *agennetos,* "unbegotten." One of their more powerful arguments is that since God the Father's nature is "unbegotten" and the Son's nature is "begotten," the Son cannot be of the same nature as the Father. See Aetius, *Syntagmation* 16-17, in Wickham, 542, 546-47, and Eunomius, *Apology* 8, 12, in Vaggione, 40-43, 46-49. For references in Eunomius's *Apology for the Apology,* see Vaggione's outline, 99-127.

14. Williams, 25, 18.

15. Socrates *H.E.* 1.36 and 2.40, *PG* 67, 172B-C and 345A. Philostorgius *H.E.* 2.14, *GCS,* 25.

of mind because his homilies are not Arian.[16] Maurice Wiles and Robert Gregg, however, insist that the better methodology is to let the ancient label of "Arian" stay in place and see what Asterius teaches. That teaching should then be included in the parameters of what Arianism was.[17]

Following their method, Arianism includes a remarkable leader who insists on the divinity of Christ and the importance of that divinity for the salvation of humankind. Asterius's theology is Christocentric; for him it is the deity of Christ that matters. Nothing in the homilies suggests an adoptionist Christology or that somehow Jesus earned his designation as the Christ. Being divine belonged to Christ by birth. Wiles and Gregg concede that there is a deficiency in Asterius's theology precisely at the point of spelling out the relationship between the Father and the Son, but it is a deficiency of silence rather than one of inappropriate statement. Asterius in these homilies does not make the relationship clear. Yet it is possible that Arians like Asterius left the exact nature of the divinity of Christ unspecified for two reasons. First, they were concerned that the orthodox claim of the Son's equality of nature with the Father, when compared to the Father, made the divinity of Christ less accessible to mankind. Second, that orthodox claim reintroduced all the problems of patripassionism that had infested earlier centuries.

Yet the kind of divinity for Christ that Asterius confesses is important because it allows him to say that God, not some mere man, suffers on the cross for our sins. Salvation is to be understood as a divine exchange in which Christ "takes flesh and gives divinity."[18] This divinization is not substantialist; it depends significantly upon moral progress marked by the obedience of the believer, but it is divinization none the less.[19] This understanding of salvation as divinization, with

16. Aloys Grillmeier, *Christ in Christian Tradition,* rev. ed., trans. John Bowden (Atlanta: John Knox, 1975), 206-14. Philostorgius *H.E.* 10.1, *GCS,* 126, hints that Asterius did change his mind.

17. Maurice Wiles, in collaboration with Robert Gregg, "Asterius: A New Chapter in the History of Arianism," *Arianism: Historical and Theological Reassessments,* 111-52.

18. Richard, 241, *Hom.* 30.7.

19. Wiles and Gregg, 111-52.

all its similarity to orthodox Alexandrian logos-sarx language, is not limited to Asterius, although it is perhaps most clear in his homilies. In the West an Arian scholion to the Council of Aquileia says, "Even in flesh like ours the impassible God, the Word, suffered and the incorruptible God endured corruption, in order that he might change our state to incorruptibility."[20] Here deep piety, words of worship, are in evidence, not some cold, careful philosophical distinctions.[21] Wiles and Gregg are willing to designate Arianism on the basis of Asterius's, homilies as "a movement, however misguided, of a religious and evangelical spirit, a movement whose heart and basic motivation was a passionate defence of the gospel of the incarnation."[22] Both the western scholion and the eastern homilies of Asterius can be faulted because they do not include more careful distinctions about the nature of the divinity of Christ. In an unexpected way, however, their depictions of Christ are not a part of the more prominent picture of Arianism that still can be found in general church history textbooks as well as some patristic surveys.

Robert Gregg and Dennis Groh, in perhaps the most stimulating and controversial study of recent years, have presented in detail a fundamental position of Arianism that is too often missed.

> We contend that early Arianism is most intelligible when viewed as a scheme of salvation. Soteriological concerns dominate the texts and inform every major aspect of the controversy. At the center of the Arian soteriology was a redeemer, obedient to his Creator's will, whose life of virtue modeled perfect creaturehood and hence the path of salvation for all Christians.[23]

20. Roger Gryson, *Scripts Arriana Latina, I: Collectio Veronensis. Scholia in Concilium Aquileiense. Fragmenta theologica rescripta,* Corpus Christianorum Series Latina LXXXVI (Turnhout: Brepols, 1982), 260, *Fr.* 20.

21. Charles Kannengiesser, "The Blasphemies of Arius: Athanasius of Alexandria, *De Synodis* 15," in *Arianism: Historical and Theological Reassessments,* 59-78, still thinks of Arianism in terms of it being primarily a philosophical school.

22. Wiles and Gregg, 140.

23. Robert Gregg and Dennis Groh, *Early Arianism — A View of Salvation* (Philadelphia: Fortress Press, 1981), x.

Reviews of their work have questioned whether there was no concern among early Arians for the problems of defending monotheism against the confession of the divinity of Christ. In that area they seem to have outrun the evidence. But their contribution is considerable and not to be put aside. Certainly one of the most important aspects of early Arians was their concern for the accessibility of salvation, the advancement theme, *prokope,* within their sense of Christology and the life of the faithful Christian. Any believer could follow Christ as the model of ascent toward spiritual perfection. Gregg's smaller study of the catechetical orations given by Cyril of Jerusalem makes it clear that Cyril saw the advancement theme as a prominent part of Arian teaching.[24] Maurice Wiles has pointed out that this theme of the accessibility of salvation was also strong in later Arian circles, particularly in the writings of Eunomius.[25]

Another major step forward in the attempt to reconfigure the sense of Arian self-definition has been the study of Arian worship, focused particularly on the existence of various Arian circles as worshiping communities rather than as philosophical schools. Thomas Kopecek, in a sensitive and penetrating article, has pointed historians to the *Apostolic Constitutions* as liturgical documents written by Neo-Arians. Although an identification of the compiler as Arian has been contested,[26] the case for it is well argued and depends on a tradition of scholarship that Kopecek now sharpens.[27] The early evidence clearly

24. Robert Gregg, "Cyril of Jerusalem and the Arians," in *Arianism: Historical and Theological Reassessments,* 85-107.

25. Maurice Wiles, "Eunomius: Hair-Splitting Dialectician or Defender of the Accessibility of Salvation," in *The Making of Orthodoxy: Essays in Honour of Henry Chadwick* (Cambridge: Cambridge University Press, 1989), 157-72.

26. In the most recent edition of the *Apostolic Constitutions,* Manfred Metzger, *Les Constitutions Apostoliques,* Tomes I-III, Sources chrétiennes 320 (1985), SC 329 (1986), and SC 336 (1987), argues against an Arian compiler, but Kopecek in his reviews of the edition, *Journal of Theological Studies,* n.s. 38 (1987): 208-11, and 39 (1988): 611-18, demonstrates the weakness of Metzger's arguments.

27. Bishop Ussher, *Polc. et Ign. ep.* (Oxford, 1644), listed a number of characteristics that made him see the recently rediscovered liturgical manual as Arian. The most compelling modern argument prior to that of Kopecek is C. H. Turner, "Notes on the Apostolic Constitutions, I. The Compiler an Arian," *Journal of Theological Studies,* o.s. 16 (1914): 54-61. D. Hagedorn, *Der Hiob-*

points in that direction. The council of Trullo in 692 insisted that the
Apostolic Constitutions had been interpolated by "heretics"; Photius
identified the interpolators as Arians.[28]

Kopecek lists five characteristics that identify the document as
Neo-Arian. First, a series of six prayers depends on "a conservative
eucharistic liturgical tradition which was pronouncedly Jewish-Christian in character."[29] Both Bousset and Fiensy have demonstrated that
these prayers are Jewish-Christian;[30] indeed the *Sanctus* of the prayer
in 7.35 has no parallel in Christian literature. Jewish monotheism
forms the basis of all the prayers. Early Arians may well not have
been so influenced by Jewish-Christianity as Rudolf Lorenz has
shown,[31] but the Neo-Arians were. Second, the subordination of
Christ to God is sharply in evidence. Not only the prayers of Book
7 but also a number of the praise forms in Book 8.5-15 highlight
that subordination. Book 8.5.1-2 follows an outline found both in
Arius's profession of faith and in similar professions of Aetius and
Eunomius. Third, it is clear from other literature that the Neo-Arians
thought of Christ in terms of his status as the "first-born of creation"
and in his role as "the creaturely prototype for the Christian's own
baptismal death and resurrection."[32] In the little over a dozen references to baptism in the *Apostolic Constitutions,* immersion is referred to as "into the death of Christ" and entails only one immersion, not the three in the name of the Father, Son, and Holy Spirit.[33]
The Son may be the high priest, but his function is that of "God's

---

kommentar des Arianers Julian (Berlin: Walter de Gruyter, 1973), xxxvii-lv, argues
that the *Clementine Homilies* are also from Arian hands.

28. Mansi 11.940c. Photius *Bibliotheca* 113.

29. *Apostolic Constitutions* 7.33-38. Kopecek, 155.

30. Wilhelm Bousset, "Eine jüdische Gebetssammlung im siebenten Buch
der apostolischen Konstitutionen," *Nachrichten von der königlichen Gesellschaft
der Wissenschaften zu Göttingen Philologishhistorsiche Klasse,* 1915 (1916), 435-89;
David Fiensy, *Prayers Alleged to Be Jewish: An Examination of the Constitutiones
Apostolorum,* Brown Judaic Studies 65 (Chico, CA: Scholars Press, 1985).

31. Lorenz, *Arius judiazans?*

32. Kopecek, 166.

33. Socrates *H.E.* 5.24, *PG* 67, 649A, also says that Arians "baptized not
into the name of the Trinity, but into the death of Christ." Philostorgius *H.E.*
10.4, *GCS,* 127, agrees.

primary worshipper."[34] Fourth, worship of the Son is rigorously restricted. God the Father is the one and only true God; the Son is not properly God. He is "the God of all sensible and intellectual nature."[35] Fifth, the *Apostolic Constitutions* "downplay affective worship in favor of self-consciously intellectual worship, a worship of intellectual assent to God's revelation of his essence and of his activity in the world, a worship of petition for additional revelation to which the Neo-Arians could assent."[36]

With these identifications we can see clearly that later Arian communities were churches, not schools; they had deeply faithful concerns that led them to take the positions that they did. Although their worship was at least at times more intellectual than affective in its approach, it was a conservative restatement of early Christian sentiments that followed particularly Jewish-Christian patterns.

Once this worshiping milieu is recognized, other snippets of Arian understandings take their place in the fuller picture. Although their best theologians did insist that the divinity of Christ must be a secondary one because of various passages in Scripture, their communities could make confessions about the passion of the impassible that perhaps by rules of logic should not have been a part of their worship services. If we had access to their hymnody and more of their sermons we might indeed find that they confessed a number of the standard phrases that at first "modern" sight seem restricted to the orthodox.

Fairness to the losers of heretical wars is vital to the writing of ecumenical church history. Modern patristic specialists have been actively describing Arianism with such values clearly in place. But two additional aspects of such ecumenical history also need to be involved in the writing of accounts concerned with Arianism and its opponents. The victors also deserve a smidgen of fairness. Athanasius did not correctly represent Arius and the early Arians in every case. He did

34. *Apostolic Constitutions* 8.12.7, 27, particularly Vatican Greek Codex 1506. Kopecek, 169.
35. *Apostolic Constitutions* 8.12.6-7, 27, 50, particularly in Vatican Greek Codex 1506. Eunomius in his *Apology* (*PG* 45.876 and Jaeger ed. 2.281) has almost identical phrasing, "The God of all sensible and intellectual essence." Kopecek, 170 and n. 35.
36. Kopecek, 172.

draw conclusions from the materials he cites that may not have been drawn by Arians themselves. He did write the biography of Antony with deep propagandistic values in place, ones that do not mark the sayings of Antony recorded in other places.[37]

The vitriolic polemics of the Arian controversy, however, were not always one-sided. We must not forget that for decades imperial favor switched back and forth from Arian to orthodox circles. Athanasius was exiled five times by the apparent winners, who were oppressive and Arian. At the council of Tyre in 335 his accusers produced a severed hand and said that Athanasius had used it in magical ceremonies; they wanted the assembly to conclude that he either had killed the fellow or had taken advantage of his corpse. To defend himself Athanasius produced the man in question with both hands intact.[38] When the Arians were "victors," they were willing to draw inferences and make charges that were every bit as scurrilous as any such conclusions and charges brought against them by the orthodox. Later Arians accused Gregory Nazianzen of being born in a hokey town, of being ugly, and of having a horrible provincial accent unworthy of high Constantinopolitan society.[39] Gregory of Nyssa derided Aetius as the slave of a woman named Ampelis and an artisan who took up the "filthy" trade of goldsmithing only to cheat people by giving them goldplated rather than solid gold jewelry.[40] The level of rhetorical abuse in these debates was quite high, although not perceptibly higher than that in the surrounding culture, with its dependence on invective as a tool of persuasion. Not even negative advertising in twentieth-century political campaigns can equal the

---

37. Athanasius, *The Life of Antony and the Letter to Marcellinus,* trans., intro. by Robert Gregg, The Classics of Western Spirituality (New York: Paulist Press, 1980), 11-13.

38. Sozomen *H.E.* 2.23 and 25, *PG* 67, 992D-996B and 1002R-1005A. Socrates *H.E.* 1.27, *PG* 67, 156B-161C.

39. Gregory Nazianzen, *Or.* 33.1-8, *PG* 36, 213A-225A.

40. Gregory of Nyssa, *Contra Eunomium,* in Werner Jaeger, ed., *Gregorii Nysseni Opera* (Leiden: E. J. Brill, 1960), 1.3. Philostorgius, the Arian historian, *H.E.* 3.15, *GCS,* 44, compassionately notes that Aetius's father had worked in a government department that supplied food for the army, had failed in that business, and had his property confiscated, evidently to cover the losses. Aetius then took up goldsmithing to support the family. Philostorgius further emphasizes Aetius's love of learning and his skill in logic.

slash-and-burn techniques of the ancient world. As demeaning as the exchanges often were, they were not as rough and rude as the derision Christian orators heaped on pagan opponents.[41]

Some modern interpreters of the debate have insisted that Athanasius was such an evil manipulator that for decades no one in the East would pay attention to his theological claims. Yet the most recent study of the papyri that form the basis for some descriptions of "evil" Athanasius demonstrates that they have been misread. It calls into question whether or not the tilting of the tables in favor of the losers of these wars has led to the overstatement of the victors' vices.[42]

The suggestion that later Arians or non-Nicenes were often urban and urbane, in contradistinction to the more rural, less urbane, and monkish orthodox, is not yet a well-developed claim. The placement in major cities of orthodox bishops with upper-class status and remarkable rhetorical educations suggests that this avenue may not be the most profitable to pursue for explaining the differences between the Nicenes and non-Nicenes, although it does throw light on individual cases.[43]

41. In her paper at the 1991 Oxford Patristic Conference, "A Topography of Heresy: Arians and Manichees in the Fourth Century," Rebecca Lyman investigated in interesting ways the level of rhetoric and polemic that marked the controversy. She particularly excoriates Athanasius for talking about Arians in terms of second- and third-century heretics and contemporary fourth-century Manichees and finds both Cyril of Jerusalem and Gregory of Nyssa to be more fair. This is an important avenue of research that needs to be broadened and deepened. A version of the paper will appear under the title "A Topography of Heresy: Mapping the Rhetorical Creation of Arianism" in Michel Barnes and Daniel H. Williams, eds., *Arianism after Arius* (Edinburgh: T. & T. Clark, forthcoming). It follows a lead she developed in "Arians and Manichees on Christ," *The Journal of Theological Studies*, n.s. 40 (1989): 493-503.

My own sense is that the issues are made more complex when the wider polemical context is drawn in. Gregory Nazianzen never attacked his Arian foes with the same vitriol he poured on the deceased Julian the "Apostate" in his Orations 4 and 5.

42. Duane Wade-Hampton Arnold, *The Early Episcopal Career of Athanasius of Alexandria* (Notre Dame, IN: University of Notre Dame Press, 1991), restudies the sources and claims that both texts and papyri have been misread when they indicate how perversely political Athanasius was.

43. Richard Paul Vaggione's "Of Monks and Lounge-Lizards: 'Arians', Polemics, and Asceticism in the Roman East," a paper given at the 1991 Oxford Patristic Conference, will appear in Barnes and Williams. Vaggione makes the

The most important question is whether or not this new depiction of the various Arian circles, with their worshiping congregational base intact, their varied positions on Christology elucidated, and their concern for salvation, recognizes demands that they be seen as developing the most adequate understanding of the incarnation, of trinity, and of Christology. Does fairness to these losers in the ecclesiastical wars require that their views be accepted as fuller and clearer than traditional orthodoxy? There is a major gain in the writing of ecumenical church history when those described as heretics are viewed more generously. Worshiping communities who made persuasive attempts to proclaim the accessibility of salvation should never be viewed as totally wrong. Certain "orthodox" views of Christ have had great difficulty seeing him as a full man who accepted the will of God for himself. But if "adequate understanding" of the incarnation means at least that more aspects of Christian scripture are brought into some

---

solid case that Arius and a group of important late non-Nicene leaders were often urbane and centered in the cities. There some of them practiced a moderate asceticism. In his view they differed from Nicene leaders, who were often radically ascetic monks from the countryside, who disliked urban ways and rejected rhetoric, the basic education of the ancient world.

In my judgment his observations about the Nicenes are not persuasively nuanced. Bishop Alexander and Athanasius were urban figures. The higher social positions of some orthodox leaders, particularly the Cappadocian fathers — Basil of Caesarea, Gregory of Nazianzus, and Gregory of Nyssa — fueled their condescending polemics against Aetius and Eunomius. They had used their wealth and prestige to study in the great urban centers of education like Alexandria, Antioch, and Athens and stood against rhetoric primarily in the sense that they used its tools to fight sophistic rhetoric in its worst forms. (I argue that Gregory Nazianzen was an adept philosophical rhetorician in *Faith Gives Fullness to Reasoning: The Five Theological Orations of Gregory Nazianzen,* Supplements to *Vigiliae Christianae* 13, intro., comm. by Frederick Norris; trans. Lionel Wickham and Frederick Williams [Leiden: E. J. Brill, 1991].) The Cappadocians attack the later Arians Aetius and Eunomius as lower-class, uneducated pretenders.

Many of the bishops who supported Nicene faith in 325 and 381 were themselves urban dwellers who stayed in the cities. In the period between the two ecumenical councils, some of them were in the countryside because they had been exiled there by non-Nicene victors who were supported by imperial power. When, however, Gregory Nazianzen resigned the presidency of the 381 Constantinopolitan council and railed against those who struck him as unvirtuous, a number of his targets were urban Nicene bishops (see particularly *Or.* 42, *PG* 36, 457A-492C, and *Carmen de vita sua* II, 1506-1904, *PG* 37, 1133-1162).

kind of coherent, more comprehensive whole, then the ancient charges of the victorious Nicenes against the defeated non-Nicenes need to be looked at yet again.

Arians made salvation accessible, defended the divinity of the Son, and worshiped in a certain kind of awe and reverence. As communities they were not primarily composed of arrogant philosophers who chided their stupid, naive opponents. Yet as Athanasius claimed in his *Discourses against the Arians* and Gregory Nazianzen claimed in his *Theological Orations,* these non-Nicenes did not find ways to appropriate the high Christologies of the New Testament, particularly what we now see as the pre-Pauline hymns of early Hellenistic Jewish-Christianity, parts of the Pauline epistles, and the Gospel of John. Athanasius chose about twenty texts that he thought the Arians misinterpreted. Gregory insisted that his Christology could explain all the passages that the Arians employed to prove that the Son was inferior or subordinate. Those verses should be attributed to either the Son in his limited, incarnate state or to the manhood. But those places within the New Testament where the Son is viewed as of the same nature as the Father were not explained by the Arians.[44]

Such issues are still debated. It is not certain that well-oriented ecumenical church history can avoid the questions of heresy and orthodoxy, of adequacy and inadequacy. Rowan Williams notes that early Arianism was probably a conservative movement that did not adapt well to the developing theology. Yet he warns that the Nicene decision to make the faith something enforced by the totalitarian power of bishops remains highly questionable.[45] On the other side Maurice Wiles, who as a modern Christian has questioned the adequacy of the conception of incarnation, notes that what is needed now is not the overthrow of the Cappadocian orthodoxy but the recognition that the Arians too were a reverent people trying to understand

44. Athanasius in his three *Discourses against the Arians, PG* 26, 12-468A, imbeds those texts in hundreds of others. *Faith Gives Fullness to Reasoning: The Five Theological Orations of Gregory Nazianzen* (n. 43 above) shows that Gregory the Theologian used over seven hundred fifty biblical verses in his battle with later Arians, Pneumatomachians, and pagans.

45. Rowan Williams, *Arius: Heresy and Tradition* (London: Darton, Longman and Todd, 1987), esp. 233-45.

the faith.[46] Both views work from stated commitments about what modern Christianity is and should be; both inform any attempt to write ecumenical history.

The entire historical study of Arianism raises in distinct profile the question of how and why people write history. Is history a positivistic, objective science in which no values or commitments drive the researchers other than their love of the truth? Or does history always involve various values and commitments? The latter is certainly the case in the investigation of Arianism, although it is not always announced by the participants. Surely there are ways to be more objective rather than less, to be more careful about reading the texts with empathy if not sympathy. But aspects of the same polemic are involved in the contemporary debates as were involved in the fourth-century debates. Maurice Wiles points out that bilateral conversations between Roman Catholics and Lutherans led by John Courtney Murray and George Lindbeck viewed the Nicene-Constantinopolitan Creed as a basic definition of Christianity. Their concern for unity between Catholics and Lutherans colored their rejection of Arianism as subordinationist in its Christology; it blinded them to Arian religious and soteriological concerns. But there is little doubt that Wiles's picture of the Arians is also colored by his view that the incarnation of God in Christ is an impossible idea, one that modern Christianity must jettison if it is to preach the good news to the contemporary world.[47]

For me the Nicene-Constantinopolitan Creed is a remarkable statement of the center of the Christian *consensus fidelium*,[48] one that

46. Wiles, 169.

47. Wiles, 158-59. Wiles's forceful sentence is: "The ecumenical usefulness of their failure to acknowledge a religious or soteriological dimension to the Arian position is only too evident." Yet in two other articles — among a number of pieces that express his views — "Christianity without Incarnation?" and "Myth in Theology," in John Hick, ed., *The Myth of God Incarnate* (Philadelphia: The Westminster Press, 1977), 1-10, 148-66, Wiles makes it crystal clear that he does not see how the Nicene doctrine of incarnation can be employed in the modern world. He, therefore, is not without his own sense of contemporary "usefulness" when he describes historical positions.

48. Rowan Williams, "Does It Make Sense to Speak of pre-Nicene Orthodoxy," in *The Making of Orthodoxy*, 1-23, offers carefully nuanced answers to that question: yes, but not as often thought. S. Mark Heim, ed., *Faith to Creed: Ecumenical Perspectives on the Affirmation of the Apostolic Faith of the Fourth*

can be followed because the churches have received it, not because the bishops in their councils have enforced it.[49] Positively the creed reflects a wider base in both scripture and tradition than what is found among Arian leaders. That is my confession, but certainly not mine alone. Thus, the adequacy of Arian theology and worship for me is determined by my understanding of that *consensus.* Yet I can also suggest that fourth-century Nicenes argued the inadequacy of Arianism on the basis of its inability to deal with as much scripture as their own hermeneutical models were able to describe.[50] That does not remove my presentation from its framework of values and commitments, but it does suggest that looking at more of the scriptural data would allow one to press the question of adequacy in yet another way. On the basis of what we have left from the Arians I think the Nicenes are more representative of the fuller Christian *consensus.* But much of the Arian work is lost, suppressed by the victors at Constantinople in 381 and beyond.

Supporters of this better nuanced understanding of Arianism, one that contemporary historical scholarship finds more representative of the texts we possess, have not yet convinced the church catholic of the adequacy of Arian or non-Nicene views for the expression of Christian faith. The ancient creeds are still the received faith of the church and thus must form a significant part of the concern for any ecumenical church history. We may at the least, however, be thankful, as Pelikan insists, that "Arianism helped to keep churchly doctrine both honest and evangelical."[51] Its defenders in the present do no less. Indeed they do more. They remind us how slowly consensus is

Century (Grand Rapids: Eerdmans, 1991), demonstrates how that creed can be important to a number of modern Christian traditions. For my own views see *The Apostolic Faith: Protestants and Roman Catholics* (Collegeville, MN: The Liturgical Press, forthcoming).

49. In *Ep.* 130, *PG* 37, 225A-B, Gregory Nazianzen, one of the architects of orthodoxy, warned his nephew to avoid councils because they were dangerous for the soul.

50. See my "Wonder, Worship and Writ: Patristic Christology," *Ex Auditu* 7 (1991): 59-72, which looks at that topic particularly in Athanasius and Gregory Nazianzen.

51. Pelikan, 200.

built, how cruelly ancient labels can be applied to contemporary Christians, and how often remarkably faithful people seem to be on the other side.[52]

52. See Rebecca Lyman, "RECKONINGS in Heresy and Orthodoxy, Ancient and Modern," *Anglican Theological Review* LXXIV (1992): 125-32.

5. Katharina Schütz Zell: A Protestant Reformer

Elsie Anne McKee

Katharina Schütz Zell (KSZ)[1] was a reformer, a devout Christian for whom the renewal of the gospel was the definitive experience of her life, empowering and shaping it in ways large and small. KSZ might be presented as a paradigmatic figure: an active urban supporter of Protestant biblical preaching, a pastor's wife and tireless friend of the afflicted, a lay writer of vernacular religious texts. All of these are true, but they reduce a most distinctive person to a type.

It is useful to bear in mind some of the ways in which KSZ is representative of the first generation of Protestant reformers. However, in order to glimpse the reform movement as a movement, it is perhaps more important to allow one person, with all her individual gifts and personal idiosyncrasies, to embody what it meant to live in the vivid, complex, exciting, and confusing first half of the sixteenth century.

In keeping with this purpose, this article is an essay, a series of

---

1. The naming of Katharina Schütz Zell presents a few problems. She is best known as Katherine Zell. She herself published under the name Schützin (feminine of her father's name) in the first years of her marriage, and used Zellin (feminine of her husband's name) later. In Strasbourg she was commonly called Schützin or "Maister Mathis fraw." When she became known beyond the bounds of Strasbourg it was as Zell(in). For simplicity, Katharina Schütz Zell is designated "KSZ" here. She was probably born in early 1498, and died 5 Sept. 1562.

73

snapshots from a moving picture. The whole film, which will provide continuity, context, and a perspective for these little photos, is in process.[2]

The Beginning

The first clear frame is a flashback.[3] An elderly woman, scarred with struggle to serve her God and her faith, her husband and her people, recalls the coming of "the gospel" to her pious, anxious young self. The old KSZ's face lights up again in remembered joy.

Young Katharina Schütz, a craftsman's daughter in early sixteenth-century Strasbourg, was well known for her religious devotion. Women gathered around her, and together they shared good works and attendance at the sacraments, but somehow nothing seemed to cure the anxiety about their salvation. KSZ was on good terms with the priests, who, like her family and neighbors, respected her piety. But again, what the priests said did not help, and she was "sick unto death."

> We were in such anxiety and worry about how to be sure of the grace of God, but in all our many works, religious practices, and sacraments of that [pre-Luther] church we never could find rest. Then God had mercy on us and on many people; He raised up and sent out the dear and now blessed Dr. Martin Luther, who by word

2. Two books are in process, a biography, *Katharina Schütz Zell: The Life and Thought of a Sixteenth-Century Reformer* (Grand Rapids: Eerdmans, forthcoming 1997-98), and a critical edition of her works, *The Writings of Katharina Schütz Zell* (Grand Rapids: Eerdmans, forthcoming 1997-98). Documentation here is minimal because full references will appear later.

3. The pictures are appropriately set as flashbacks, since most of KSZ's autobiographical comments come from correspondence published as *Ein Brieff an die gantze Burgerschafft der Statt Strassburg/von Katherina Zellin/dessen jetz säligen Matthei Zellen/dess alten und ersten Predigers des Evangelii diser Statt/nachgelassne Ehefraw/Betreffend Herr Ludwigen Rabus/jetz ein Prediger der Statt Ulm/sampt zweyen brieffen ir und sein/die mag mengklich lesen und urtheilen on gunst und hassz/sonder allein der warheit warnemen. Dabey auch ein sanffte antwort/auff jeden Artickel/seines brieffs* (Strasbourg, 30 Dec. 1557). (Hereafter *Ein Brieff*; see nn. 29-30 for context.)

and writing set out the loving Lord Jesus Christ in such a lovely way that I thought I had been drawn up out of the depths of the earth, indeed out of grim bitter hell into the dear sweet heaven.[4]

There were two critical elements in KSZ's conversion. First was a new sense of trust in Christ the Lamb, who alone was worthy to open the book with seven seals (Rev. 5:1ff.) and give peace in her heart, by the gracious gift of faith, without reference to her merits. The other was a new understanding of the teaching of scripture, which had been like a closed book when she read it earlier.[5] The result was that KSZ applied to herself Christ's words to Peter: "I will make you a fisher of people," and she struggled day and night to understand and act on this call.[6]

KSZ's thoughts move swiftly to the next picture. The immediate visible fruit of Katharina Schütz's conversion was . . . marriage to the cathedral priest Matthew Zell!

At first glance this might hardly seem an act of faith, but in 1523 it was clearly an affirmation of commitment to the gospel for a respectable young woman from a good guild family. Matthew Zell was the first established priest in Strasbourg to follow Martin Luther, and throughout his life Zell remained the most popular of the city's Protestant preachers. The marriage of priests caused quite a stir, since it represented a point of no return in the rejection of canon law, and thus of the authority of the church's tradition, in the name of the pure Word of God. The struggle between the bishop, in whose diocese Strasbourg lay, and the city council, which protected the married priests, brought the break with the medieval church to a head.

That laypeople as well as the bishop regarded clerical marriage as notable is evident in the number of references to the Zells and other

---

4. *Ein Brieff,* esp. A2r-A3r; quotation A3r. Translating KSZ is rather difficult, since often her writing is very condensed, and one word or phrase may be dependent on or related to several others. In such cases I have expanded the text slightly.

5. The second description of KSZ's conversion comes from a long manuscript letter (or short treatise) dated 19 Oct. 1553. It is found in the Strasbourg archives (AST 76, 46). See folios 9v, 11v, 12r.

6. *Ein Brieff,* A3r.

clerical couples in contemporary letters and chronicles. Laypeople, however, tended to approve of their priests becoming honest husbands and citizens rather than often scandalous servants of a "foreign" authority. Ordinary people, especially among the poorer guilds, were enthusiastic about the new biblical preaching that so greatly changed KSZ's life. Even the aristocracy had an ambivalent attitude toward the clergy, whose first earthly allegiance was not to the city. Thus, changes favored by religious enthusiasm were fueled also by an old anti-clericalism.[7]

Married clergy soon became a normal part of Strasbourg's church life, but this does not mean that the early years of the Zells' marriage were easy. The courage of the women who married priests was not as often appreciated as that of their husbands, and they usually shared the ignominy without the praise. The elderly KSZ grins: shortly after she and Matthew were married, she had written a "hot letter" to the bishop, defending clerical marriage; and after some controversy, she published a version of it. KSZ roundly affirmed the biblical character of priestly marriage, and denied the slanderous rumors about the Zells' own motives for marrying and the conduct of their household.[8]

The smile deepens, as the elderly woman thinks of her husband, but the tears come also. The marriage of Katharina Schütz and Matthew Zell was a resounding success — as a partnership fully as much as a marriage. Both partners were unusual people, but one important factor in their union was their common understanding of vocation. For both Zells, the calling was to be faithful servants of the gospel.

7. See W. Stafford, *Domesticating the Clergy: The Inception of the Reformation in Strasbourg, 1522-1524* (Missoula, MT: Scholars Press, 1976); T. A. Brady, *Ruling Class, Regime, and the Reformation at Strasbourg 1520-1555* (Leiden: E. J. Brill, 1978), esp. ch. 6.

8. For references to the "hot letter" in Strasbourg government proceedings, see Brant, "Annales," *Bulletin de la Société pour la Conservation des Monuments Historiques d'Alsace* (= BSCMHA) 19 (1899), #4501, 4540. The city council got word (in Feb. 1524) of KSZ's "hot" letter and told Matthew Zell to prevent her publishing it, but KSZ went ahead; and the next notice (Sept. 1524) indicates that the council prohibited such attacks (instituted censorship, essentially). The published text is entitled *Entschuldigung Katharina Schützinn/für M. Matthes Zellen/iren Eegemahel/der ein Pfarrher und dyener ist im wort Gottes zuo Strassburg. Von wegen grosser lügen uff in erdiecht* (Strasbourg [?], 1524). (Hereafter *Entschuldigung.*)

As KSZ later said, she would not have married Matthew if she had not agreed with his faith, and they never in their lives disagreed in matters of faith — or even other things. KSZ said that Matthew himself did not marry her for beauty or wealth (neither of which she possessed in any significant measure), but for the sake of her zeal and action and faith.[9]

KSZ's memories turn lovingly to the ministry she had shared with her husband. She recalls that their marriage vows had nothing to do with money but with vocation; Matthew charged Katharina to be mother to all the afflicted. But this was not all. Matthew called Katharina his *"Helffer"* (assistant minister), and she proudly affirmed that she had been the best assistant he ever had. (This was in fact probably true, but it certainly was not sweet to the ears of Matthew's ordained male assistant to whom she wrote it!) Not only had Matthew cheerfully accepted household inconveniences caused by KSZ's pastoral duties in parish and city, but he even encouraged her in these activities.[10]

KSZ said that she had never mounted the pulpit — that was not necessary for her vocation, and not appropriate for a Christian woman. However, apostasy and preaching from the pulpit (the place is important: KSZ did not refrain from preaching informally elsewhere) are the only two specifics that KSZ mentions as unsuitable for a Christian woman, and this left considerable space for her exercise of her ministry.[11]

KSZ affirmed repeatedly that Matthew approved of her faith, understanding, and actions, while she herself obeyed his command because she regarded the things that he asked her to do as being in accord with God's commandment. KSZ sometimes summed up her

9. See *Ein Brieff,* G4v, H1r, J3r; *Entschuldigung,* B7r-v. 1553 letter, 2r.

10. See *Ein Brieff,* G4v-H1r, G2v, A2r-v. KSZ speaks of herself in a number of ways; two are "church mother" (A2v) and "fellow-worker" (with the first reformers, F1v). See n. 39. For further discussion, see McKee, *Katharina Schütz Zell.*

11. See *Ein Brieff,* G2v, H3r; see below at n. 21 on preaching. "Preaching from the pulpit" is essentially equivalent to ordination, which KSZ believed scripture teaches is an office for men, though she objects vigorously to the way some men exercise the office. She says that she, like Anna, knows scripture well enough to teach it, and hints that she could preach better than those who slander others from the pulpit. See 1553 letter, 5r-v.

service to the members of the church under the categories of speaking, writing, and acting.[12] A sketch of these facets of her work will be followed by a brief consideration of some of the theological convictions that guided the Zells' lives.

The Speaking, Writing, and Acting of KSZ

The speaking, writing, and acting of KSZ's vocation present a whole series of snapshots. Most are fairly traditional, but others are of a character to raise eyebrows and produce bursts of applause or fits of temper, depending on the viewer's perspective.

One of KSZ's best known and probably most time-consuming roles was that of mother of the afflicted, mother in the church. Not only was her home a kind of ever-expanding hostel, but also KSZ was one of the moving spirits in galvanizing Strasbourg's amazing hospitality to refugees of all descriptions. The Zells themselves were constantly taking in people, finding food and shelter and jobs. They also spent a considerable amount of time and money coming and going on charitable errands of all sorts. Religious refugees were a specialty, but one did not need to agree with the Zells' faith in order to benefit from their kindness.[13]

In a measure, Matthew 25:31-44 might be taken as KSZ's model text for one major part of her life's work. Visits to prisoners — both "heretics" and common criminals — were a natural activity. More frequent was the work with the sick and poor, whether refugees or family members, parishioners or homeless children. Even as an elderly widow, KSZ was still taking in anyone who came to her, and supporting and caring for poor children and abandoned orphans, all at her own expense.[14] Alongside the physical care was the daily counseling of

12. See *Ein Brieff*, H2v, H1r, H3r, G2r, J3r.
13. See *Ein Brieff*, esp. G2r-G3r *et passim* and below n. 33.
14. See *Ein Brieff*, A2v, D2r, G2v-G3r, H2r, N5r-v *et passim;* various of KSZ's letters, e.g., to Pellican, 4 Jan. 1549, and 1553 letter, 2r-v, 5v. For examples of "heretics" and criminals, see Brant, "Annales," BSCMHA 19 (1899), #4924, 5021. For orphans, see *Quellen der Taufer Geschichte* (QTG) 16, #1686. On poor relief, see O. Winckelmann, *Das Fürsorgewesen der Stadt Strassburg* (Leipzig, 1922).

neighbors and fellow citizens, or even people in other cities. Comfort and correction, encouragement and instruction were a part of the care for the afflicted; and KSZ wrote to those whom she could not visit in person.[15]

KSZ set high standards for herself and her fellow Christians. Or rather, she believed these standards were set by the gospel, and she was critical of herself and others when she or they failed to measure up to the true Christian life.[16] The point was not to earn salvation; no one shares in Christ's office of savior. However, all are called to share in his office of love, to live as befits the members of his body.[17] There was no space in KSZ's ideal for idle pleasures: dancing and fancy dress, self-indulgence, or laziness in serving God and the neighbor. KSZ measured men and women alike by Christ and the apostles, and approved or corrected appropriately. The gospel is equally compelling for all believers, and faithfulness has no gender. Day and night one is "on call" as a Christian.

This does not mean that there was no recreation. Real refreshment is found in studying and talking of matters of the kingdom of God. Like other pastors' wives, KSZ had a steady stream of reformers among her house guests. She delighted in their religious discussions, and was quite ready to join in the talk. She may well have participated

15. KSZ's first publication was a letter of consolation to the Protestant women of a nearby town. The men of Kentzingen had gone with their pastor to protect him when he was forced to leave the city and then could not return to their homes when their Roman Catholic rulers seized the city. KSZ took in the refugees, and then wrote to their wives. This pastoral letter is entitled *Den leydenden Christglaubigen weybern der gemain zuo Kentzingen, meinen mit schwestern in Christo Jhesu zuo handen* ([Augsburg]: Ulhart, 1524). For various evidences of KSZ as counselor, comforter, instructor, see *Ein Brieff,* G2v-G3r, A3v, B3r, N3v, and below nn. 23ff.

16. For KSZ's self-criticism, see *Ein Brieff,* H2v; *Klag,* 5v (for full information on this sermon-memoir, see below n. 21), reference in Bucer's correspondence (letter to Oswald Myconius, before 16 July 1548). For examples of general criticism of others, *Ein Brieff,* G2r-v, N4r-v *et passim.* More specific criticism of Rabus is discussed in Elsie Anne McKee, "The Defense of Schwenckfeld, Zwingli, and the Baptists by Katharina Schütz Zell," in *Reformiertes Erbe: Festschrift für Gottfried W. Locher zu seinem 80. Geburtstag,* ed. H. A. Oberman, E. Saxer, A. Schindler, and H. Stucki (Zurich: TVZ, 1992), Band 1, 245-64.

17. See *Ein Brieff,* J1v; also *Den Psalmen,* A4v-A5r (full information on this pamphlet in n. 24).

more than most reformers' wives, in part because Matthew was in the
habit of talking over his pastoral concerns with her, but also in part
because KSZ herself was an active student of both the Bible and the
reformers' writings.[18] KSZ's conversation partners were not only reformers, however. According to a humorous note in the diary of a
genial Strasbourg Roman Catholic priest, Jacques von Gottesheim,
KSZ invited him to dinner "in order to dispute with him."[19]

KSZ not only enjoyed theological discussions in her home, she
also went elsewhere seeking them. She both corresponded with reformers and often accompanied her elderly husband in his travels to
various Protestant centers. Good friends like Wolfgang Capito sometimes commented wryly on KSZ's wish to associate with the great
leaders of the faith, but it was a respectful and often even affectionate
criticism. Though they saw her faults, her husband's colleagues did
implicitly accept her also as a colleague in serving the gospel.[20]

Perhaps two of the clearest examples of the acceptance that the
first generation accorded KSZ's "speaking out" are events related to
the deaths of Matthew Zell and Caspar Hedio. At Zell's funeral in
January 1548, Martin Bucer preached in both Latin and German, and
KSZ preached an impromptu sermon herself — which chroniclers
noted with approval and someone even considered important enough
to copy down and preserve, probably substantially as it was given.[21]

18. See *Ein Brieff,* A3v, F2v, H2r, H2v-H3r, J3r, L2r. On KSZ's study, see
nn. 24ff.
19. See Jacques von Gottesheim, "Diarium seu Ephemerides," BSCMHA
19 (1899), 272.
20. See *Ein Brieff,* A3r-v, G3r-v. Although much correspondence is lost, a
few letters give examples of KSZ's theological exchanges; KSZ wrote to Luther
about the arguments on the Lord's Supper after the Marburg colloquy (the letter
is lost but his answer of 24 Jan. 1531 exists, WA Br 6:26), to Conrad Pellican
about the Interim (4 Jan. 1549, McKee, *The Writings of KSZ*). Letters between
Bucer and the Blaurers discuss KSZ's involvement in arguments over Schwenckfeld
and whether or not the church should have godparents (9 July 1533 and 3 Feb.
1534 Bucer to Margareta; 16 Nov. 1533 and 8 Jan. 1534 Bucer to Ambrose,
QTG, 8, #406, 502, 455, 488). For Capito's comments, see letters to Neobolus
of 10 March and 13 Aug. 1538 (QTG, 15, #814, 839a). Despite criticism, in
each case there is also great respect, and this continues in later correspondence.
21. KSZ's sermon was given on 11 Jan. 1548, the day after her husband's
death. There is preserved a manuscript entitled *Klag red und Ermahnung,* which
seems to be the substance of her sermon. It is not clear exactly how the sermon

Several years later, the last of Strasbourg's four major leaders, Hedio, lay on his deathbed. Capito, Zell, Bucer were gone, but KSZ, who had ministered at many deathbeds, was still alive, and Hedio insisted that she remain with him to the end, in preference to the other preachers available in Strasbourg in 1552.[22]

Learning, both in private and from teachers of the church, was not enough for KSZ. Her task was also to teach others — primarily women and children, but she was quite ready to instruct or help men if they needed it. One of the Zells' concerns was religious education. Ignorance is not the only problem; wrong teaching and immorality must also be rooted out. Matthew Zell concentrated his attention on preaching and catechizing; KSZ turned to the home education of children and adults. She maintained that biblically inspired hymns are not merely songs, but also prayers, praise, and doctrine (teaching). So KSZ edited a collection of hymns found in a hymnbook of the Bohemian Brethren, because the contents impressed her by their biblical character. Not only plowmen in the field but also maids washing dishes or mothers with fretful babies should sing their faith, and replace the old immoral songs with ones about Christ and the true way to live.[23]

---

was preserved. The style is authentically that of KSZ, and it seems probable that she was involved in the written redaction. This may have been a kind of memoir form, which she wrote after the sermon itself. See chronicles by Specklin, and Saladin, BSCMHA 14 (1890), #2386, and BSCMHA 23 (1906), 354, for references to both Bucer's and KSZ's sermons. In March 1562, and again in June 1562, KSZ preached at the burials of two sisters, who were followers of Schwenckfeld. The fullest information is available for Felicitas Scher (June). The city preacher who was to do the funeral said that if he did the funeral, he would have to include in his comments that this woman had fallen away from the faith. The widower, Dr. Johann Winther von Andernach, thereupon asked KSZ (instead of a city preacher) to conduct the burial.

22. See *Ein Brieff,* G4r.

23. KSZ's hymnbook was made up of four inexpensive little booklets, the first entitled *Von Christo Jesu unserem säligmacher/seiner Menschwerdung/ Geburt/Beschneidung/etc. etlich Christliche und trostliche Lobgsäng* . . . (Strasbourg: Jacques Froehlich, 1534-36) *(Lobgsäng).* The comments are from the foreword in the first booklet (1534), A1v-A3v. For a full discussion of the hymnbook's contents, see Elsie Anne McKee, *Reforming Popular Piety in Sixteenth-Century Strasbourg: Katharina Schütz Zell and Her Hymnbook,* Studies in Reformed Theology and History 3:1 (Princeton: Princeton Theological Seminary, 1995).

Scripture was the central authority for KSZ: scripture as explained by the preachers, and scripture as understood through its application to her own life. On one occasion, in response to a request from some women in Speyer for help in their spiritual problems, KSZ turned to the traditional catechetical tool of the Lord's Prayer to teach, console, and comfort. Another time she shared with an elderly friend some meditations on the Psalms that she had written for herself at a time of great grief and temptation or affliction (*"anfechtung"* — possibly the deaths of her young children).[24]

The source of much of KSZ's knowledge was the teaching of Luther, Zell, and others, for she was a diligent and voracious reader.[25]

24. The exposition of the Lord's Prayer for the two women of Speyer was written in 1532. The meditations on the Psalms may have been written in these same years. A selection of the Psalms and the Lord's Prayer were published as words of comfort for a long-time Strasbourg friend of KSZ's who was living the final years of his life in isolation because he had "leprosy." Even his daughter was forbidden to visit Felix Armbruster (or Erstein), but KSZ visited as often as her own enfeebled health would allow. She published the texts to comfort her friend and others who might be in similar distress. This devotional book, the second longest of KSZ's writings, is entitled *Den Psalmen Miserere/mit dem Khünig David bedacht/gebettet/und paraphrasirt von Katharina Zellin . . . sampt dem Vatter unser mit seiner erklärung/zuogeschickt dem Christlichen mann Juncker Felix Armbruster/zum trost in seiner kranckheit/und andern angefochtenen hertzen und Concientzen/der sund halben betrüebt &c. in truck lassen kommen* (1558) *(Den Psalmen)*. For references to "visitation" see below at nn. 25-26. For the possibility that the cause was her children's deaths, see KSZ's letter to Ambrose Blaurer, 30 Sept. 1534 (McKee, *Katharina Schütz Zell*).

25. It has often been assumed that what made KSZ remarkable was her life, and that is certainly part of the truth. However, the extent of KSZ's biblical and theological knowledge has sometimes been neglected, while her general education has occasionally been overstated. (She did not know much Latin.) KSZ was not formally trained in theology or even in the humanist disciplines, but she read and wrote German fluently, and understood more theology than she has usually been credited with. KSZ knew well the preaching of the Strasbourg theologians, and she also heard many others during her visits in Switzerland and other parts of Germany. She actually refers to or cites the books of quite a number of reformers: Luther, Schwenckfeld, Brenz, Bucer, "Bellius" (Castellio), Staupitz, Melanchthon, Zwick, Bugenhagen, Savonarola, Amsdorf, Osiander, Bullinger, Gwalther, Flacius Illyricus, plus the various others included in the German translation of Castellio's *De Haereticis* (Erasmus, Franck, Calvin, Brunfels, Agricola, Pellican, Rhegius, Curio), and others less known. She also refers to some church fathers (Ambrose, Augustine, Chrysostom, Jerome, Lactantius) whom she prob-

But all was assimilated and personally recast through her own regular Bible study and meditation and through her own experience of the "visitation of God." What she learned, she then passed on to others, as she explained to her elderly friend afflicted with "leprosy."

> While I have experienced so many afflictions (temptations) [*anfectung*] in myself and in others, yet God has given me much comfort and help. I have thought of your *anfechtung* and the words of Paul, where he says "God afflicts us so that we may believe the afflicted, and comforts us again that we may be able to comfort the afflicted out of [our own] experience" [cf. 2 Cor. 1:6]. So I wanted to dedicate these two Psalms [51 and 130] to you and share them with you. Though I hope that God may give you more teaching and help in bearing your cross than I can here, yet love does not cease to care [for others because it trusts that God is acting] — like the dear Marys, who first wanted to anoint the Lord when He was already resurrected and had no more wounds [cf. Mark 16:1, Luke 23:56–24:1]. May the Lord Christ give that to you, that your pain may all be healed by the grace of God, and you may be happy and comforted and resurrected in God, without any wounds in your conscience. Still, though, I hope that God and you will not despise my work of love [this book of comfort which I offer].[26]

At times her friends poked gentle fun at KSZ's theological ambitions; not all were as supportive as Matthew Zell. Most often, however, the Strasbourg theologians' irritations were caused by KSZ's disagreement with them (as in the argument over Caspar Schwenckfeld or the practice of having godparents) and not by any fundamental objection to her theological study or any question of her integrity.

Essentially, among the first-generation reformers in Strasbourg, theological disputes remained disagreements among colleagues. By the second generation, in a situation rendered precarious by Protestant

---

ably knew only at second hand. She thinks most highly of the "first and best books," i.e., especially those from the 1520s and 1530s. In addition, KSZ also knew and read opponents of the Protestant movement: Cochläus, Murner, Treger, et al. Full discussion is given in McKee, *Katharina Schütz Zell.* For references to her life-long study, see 1553 letter, 5r; *Ein Brieff,* N4v; *Den Psalmen,* A8r-v.

26. *Den Psalmen,* A6v-A7r. KSZ also refers to "visitations" in *Ein Brieff,* E3r.

defeats, which led to increased Catholic power (the Interim), and growing confessional cleavages within the Protestant movement, KSZ's faith and practice came to be differently interpreted.[27] In many ways, KSZ remained all her life a first-generation reformer, a Protestant of the 1520s. Accommodation to the narrowing confessional boundaries and to the increasing institutionalization of the gospel, compromises with old errors, seemed to the elderly, lonely KSZ a betrayal of the hard work of the first reformers, almost even a betrayal of the gospel.[28]

27. The Interim was a religious and political reversal for Protestants, following Emperor Charles V's defeat of the Protestant Schmaldkald League in 1547. Roman Catholic worship and clergy were reestablished in defeated Protestant territories. Sometimes the control was total, as in the military reconquest of the resisting city of Constance. By considerable negotiations, which did not meet with the approval of all the citizens — some felt they should defend their faith to the death — Strasbourg managed to retain Protestant worship in certain city churches after the Interim provisions took effect in early 1550. However, the situation remained extremely tense for the nearly ten years before Protestants regained full control. During and following the Interim, Strasbourg clergy gradually moved their allegiance further and further from the early ties with the Swiss reformers, until the 1598 ecclesiastical revisions marked the city's exclusive alignment with Lutheranism and rejection of Zwinglians and Calvinists as worse than Rome. For an overview of the changing situation, see L. J. Abray, *The People's Reformation: Magistrates, Clergy, and Commons in Strasbourg, 1500-1598* (Oxford: Basil Blackwell, 1985), esp. ch. 5-6.

28. The early years of the Protestant Reformation were characterized by a strong focus on the inner and spiritual, in preference to, or sometimes even over against the outer and institutional, and by a much greater sense of openness to varied expressions of evangelical teaching. Partly this was a reaction to medieval doctrine and practice, partly it was owed to the conviction that following scripture would naturally lead everyone in the same direction and thus strict definitions were not necessary. KSZ continued to be a Protestant of the 1520s in the sense that she never really moved away from the more spiritual focus and wider view of what could be encompassed within a true expression of the faith. This does not mean that KSZ ever thought one could abandon the church or preaching, nor that everyone was equally correct. (See the discussion on the Zells' theology below.) It did mean that she objected to what she saw as taking authority from Christ and giving it to something else, such as the water in baptism. One example of a compromise with old errors that upset KSZ was the reintroduction of a form of "emergency baptism," an insistence that a child who does not receive the sacrament of baptism is damned — as if the water had the power to save. See *Ein Brieff,* H3v-H4r, where KSZ calls the early Reformation teachings of Luther and others on baptism to witness against Rabus and his friends.

KSZ leans back in her chair, with a sigh of discouragement, then straightens up with a fierce determination not to give up as long as she lives. So much change! The old and the new form such a contrast.

The focus of the problem, for KSZ, was the Zells' foster son and Matthew Zell's assistant and successor, Ludwig Rabus.[29] Rabus and his colleagues regarded many of KSZ's old friends, both living and dead, as heretics, and what was perhaps even worse in KSZ's view, they preached such slander from the pulpit, to the dismay and confusion of simple people and the discredit of their own vocation. Caspar Schwenckfeld, Ulrich Zwingli and his associates, the "Baptist brethren" (Anabaptists) — all came under fire, and KSZ herself suffered for defending them. After some years of verbal interchanges and sporadic correspondence, the whole dispute came to a head in 1557. Rabus had left Strasbourg without giving notice. Many Strasbourg citizens besides KSZ were upset, but the latter felt obliged to rebuke her foster son. When she received Rabus's insulting response, accusing her of apostasy and causing trouble in the church, KSZ decided to publish the correspondence, as an *apologia* for the earliest reformers and for her own faith and practice. The book understandably angered Rabus and some of his friends, but it received a remarkably favorable reception from others of KSZ's contemporaries.[30]

29. Ludwig Rabus (1524-1592), was born in Memmingen, educated in Wittenburg and Tübingen, where he received his doctorate in April 1553. He served as Matthew Zell's assistant 1544-48 in the Strasbourg cathedral, then was elected Zell's successor; he moved to Ulm at the end of 1556 to become the superintendent of that church. For a sketch of Rabus, see R. Kolb, *For All the Saints: Changing Perceptions of Martyrdom and Sainthood in the Lutheran Reformation* (Macon, GA: Mercer University Press, 1987), ch. 2; for a full discussion of the argument between KSZ and Rabus, see McKee, "Defense."

30. The correspondence published in *Ein Brieff* is made up of a number of letters from KSZ and one from Rabus. The earliest of KSZ's date from the end of 1555 and early 1556 and have to do primarily with her defense of Schwenckfeld. In 1557 she wrote to Rabus in Ulm concerning his secret departure. He answered briefly, and she wrote a long commentary and rebuttal of his letter. KSZ published this correspondence, with a dedicatory letter to the city of Strasbourg, appealing to these neighbors who had known her all her life, and known Rabus's behavior, to judge who had indeed acted faithfully. An anonymous reply was written to defend Rabus, but even some of his friends did not admire his behavior, and chroniclers in Strasbourg record the popular sentiment of approval for KSZ's work. See McKee, "Defense."

Theology: Faith, "Tolerance," Christian Love, and Vocation

The film moves from pictures to a kind of stream-of-consciousness musing, as the elderly but still determined KSZ considers the principles that guided her life. At the root of KSZ's problem with Rabus was the Zells' understanding of Christian faith and its confession, Christian charity and its practice.

Fundamental to both Zells was the conviction that there is a necessary "chief point" in the faith, and therefore there are certain essential elements of Christian doctrine and certain corresponding boundaries. For the Zells, "the high, true and necessary chief point [is] that Jesus is the Christ and the Son of God, and therefore He alone is the only Savior [*Seligmacher*] of all flesh."[31] (The knowledge of this chief point is found in the "gospel," the pure Word of God.) The Zells, like other Protestants, were convinced that believing in Christ as the only savior meant rejecting the teaching of the papal church; there is no place in true faith for anything that would usurp the sole salvific role of Christ, and no human works can be added to Christ's saving work.

However, among those who share the chief point, there may well be differences on lesser matters, such as church polity. Anything that hints at a return to the old bondage to human works or ceremonies must be fought; KSZ is quite firm that the weeds of false teaching, such as emergency baptism, which were rooted out by the first reformers, must never be allowed to grow again. Nonetheless, this struggle against error is directed against doctrines, not individuals; and it must be not be carried on by coercion, because faith is a gift and cannot be compelled. Preaching and verbal arguments are fair and appropriate means to proclaim the gospel, but force is ruled out.[32]

---

31. See *Ein Brieff,* D3v, E1r, F3r (quotation), G2r, K4r-v for references to "chief point." For full discussion, see McKee, "Defense."

32. KSZ approves the fact that Jews are not forced to convert (in Germany), because faith is God's gift and cannot be compelled. She uses this point in arguing that (Ana)Baptists and others also should not be harried as Rabus keeps urging the magistrates to do; *Ein Brieff,* D3v-D4r. See the reference to arguments with Roman Catholic Jacques von Gottesheim, n. 19, for KSZ's way of dealing with any Roman Catholic who would agree to discuss faith. It is important to note

(Christian rulers have a role in church affairs, but they may not convert by civil power.)

The Zells' understanding of the chief point of the faith provided a clear basis for their firm support of the gospel, but it also led them to recognize as brothers and sisters in the faith a wide spectrum of people, not all of whom even their first-generation colleagues were ready to accept. When disputes divided Schwenckfeld and the Strasbourg preachers, KSZ maintained that she found the chief point on both sides and therefore refused to part from either side, but remained in fellowship with both. In fact, she continued to uphold this stance not only against pressure from the Strasbourg establishment, but also against pressure from Schwenckfeld's followers on the other side. Fellowship with both meant precisely that — a defense of her duty to remain in contact with both, not with only one or the other. KSZ's friendship with both sides was not a matter of expediency or weakness; it was an expression of sincere conviction, held at the cost of being misinterpreted and attacked at times by both sides.[33]

Combined with their relatively unusual religious openness was the Zells' — especially KSZ's — even more wide-ranging charity. Anyone in need was welcome to their aid. As KSZ said:

[Matthew] daily commanded me, and so often said to me, that everyone should have access to him, and all who believe and confess Christ as the true Son of God and only savior of all people — let them be whoever they may — should be received at his [Zell's] table and share his roof: he will also share with them in heaven. And so,

---

that, for KSZ, the weeds to be rooted out were errors of doctrine and *not* people, because the parable of the wheat and the tares was often used as a proof text for persecuting "heretics." See S. Schwantès, "L'ivraie et les hérétiques," *Conscience et liberté* 25 (1983), 47-52.

33. *Ein Brieff,* K4r-v, for dispute between Schwenckfeld and the first-generation Strasbourgers. KSZ is often interpreted as a Schwenckfelder, pure and simple, but this is at least partially the result of inadequate information (as well as polemical highlighting of only one part of the evidence). KSZ's 1553 letter to Rabus is in fact an argument on two fronts. On one hand (3v-7r), KSZ defends herself to Rabus and his friends for maintaining her ties with Schwenckfeld. On the other hand, in the rather longer (7v-12r) and generally unknown section, KSZ explains the charges that Schwenckfelders have brought against her, primarily concerned with her refusal to break with the established Strasbourg church and with her theological independence.

at his wish and according to his good pleasure, I [KSZ] have taken their part in speech and writing, whether they were followers of our dear Dr. Luther or Zwingli or Schwenckfeld, and the poor Baptist brethren, rich and poor, wise and foolish, according to the word of St. Paul [cf. Gal. 3:28?], all might come to us. What did their names matter to us? We were not obliged to share the ideas and faith of anyone, but were obligated to show to each one love, service, and mercy as our teacher Christ has taught us [cf. Matt. 5:43].[34]

It is small wonder that KSZ, one of the few survivors of the outspoken first generation, should appear to the narrowing confessionalism of the post-1550 theologians as indiscriminate in her religious views and soft-headed in her religious practice.

Along with KSZ's passionate attachment to scripture and the gospel, as taught by the first-generation reformers, she had a moderate but confident assurance of the power of God in lay Christians. Throughout her life KSZ respected and deferred to preachers of the gospel — not because they were ordained but because they were particularly learned in the scripture and called to feed the people the food necessary for their salvation, that is, to preach the word of God.[35] KSZ did not automatically assume that everyone is an equally good expositor of the Bible.

However, when the learned fail to listen to God's will, when pastors lead people astray by shouting polemic rather than scripture from the pulpit, then God uses donkeys to rebuke prophets. From her earliest writings to the end, KSZ's favorite image for her own authority in *polemical* situations was Balaam's ass. Convinced that she was following scripture in defending clerical marriage, KSZ defied the bishop even as the donkey rebuked Balaam.[36]

Many years later, with a far greater knowledge of the Bible on

34. See *Ein Brieff,* H2v.

35. *Den Psalmen,* G5r-G6v, gives a description of the preacher's role in protecting people by feeding them the word of God. The 1553 letter, 9v-11r, expresses at length the importance of preachers (those who know how to proclaim the gospel — not necessarily those with theological degrees).

36. See *Entschuldigung,* C3r. Others use the image of Balaam, too, though not all in the same way. KSZ probably was drawn to the image by Luther's use of it in his treatise *To the Christian Nobility of the German Nation,* WA 6:412, but she develops the idea. See McKee, *Katharina Schütz Zell.*

which to draw, KSZ still used this image in her arguments with Rabus. It is characteristic of KSZ, however, that now she identifies herself not only with the biblical figures but also with the first reformers. In one letter, KSZ compares Rabus's relationship to Schwenckfeld with the Roman Catholic treatment of Luther. Rabus, like Balaam and Luther's opponents, has his eyes closed. As for KSZ, she, like the donkey (and Luther!), sees truly, and she will bless what Rabus curses.[37] In a later letter, KSZ notes that it was the business of Rabus's fellow preachers to correct him, and she had waited for them. If they had done so, she would not have been obliged to write as she has, but could have kept silence. Since, however, the preachers have not done their own work, she appeals to Christ's words to the Jews (Luke 19:40): " 'If these [crowds] kept silent, the stones would have to cry out.' I [KSZ] am, however, more than a stone. Let me be Balaam's donkey, who saw the angel with the sword standing in the way, whom the prophet did not see."[38]

One of the notable points in KSZ's defense of lay inspiration is her clear acceptance of the importance of learning, both personally studying the Bible and learning from those who have studied scripture "professionally." There is an authority in the knowledge of the word of God that was not found in the ordination and teachings of the old church. In fact, KSZ claimed her own authority in good part because she was learned in the scriptures. Inspiration for her was not new revelation. At one point KSZ (alluding probably to Luther's sarcastic comment on those visionaries who swallowed the Holy Spirit, feathers and all), exclaims humorously that she has never seen, never mind received, one feather of the Holy Spirit! Especially in later years, KSZ's favorite image for her own teaching role was the aged prophetess Anna, who saw the Christ in the temple and praised God and proclaimed the Lord to all who were looking for the hope of Israel (cf. Luke 2:36-38).[39]

Always grateful for the aid of others more learned in the Bible

37. *Ein Brieff,* L4r-v.
38. *Ein Brieff,* F1v.
39. For the Holy Spirit's feathers, see Luther, *Against the Heavenly Prophets,* WA 18:66 (cf. 152); KSZ, 1553 letter, 3r. The image builds on the traditional representation of the Holy Spirit as a dove; Luther is ridiculing those who claim that they know the mind of the Spirit apart from scripture — by having "swallowed" the Spirit. For KSZ's references to herself as Anna, see 1553 letter, 5r (see above at n. 11); *Ein Brieff,* N4r, A2r.

than she, KSZ nevertheless retained her independence. Constantly in
the dispute with Rabus, KSZ calls upon both scripture and the "first
and best books" of the great reformers, which she knew remarkably
well; she even makes occasional references to leaders of the early
church, although these are almost certainly secondhand knowledge.
Yet KSZ consistently refused to move away from the gospel preaching
that had lifted her from hell to heaven.

> So I also say, Luther, Zwingli, Schwenckfeld and all good teachers
> and preachers, together with the prophets and apostles, did not
> become a sacrifice on the cross for me, but Christ the Son of God
> Himself. Why should I want to call myself by their names? None of
> them wanted that, either, but spoke and wrote against it. However,
> should I then deny, should I not confess what great gifts God has
> given, and what good God has done through Peter, Paul, John, and
> other apostles, and also in our time through Luther, Zwingli,
> Schwenckfeld, Capito, Bucer, Hedio, Zell, and so many outstanding
> learned people and preachers in Germany? No, that I will not allow
> on anyone's account. But I also do not want to be called after them
> or by their names, but only to be called a Christian, after my only
> Lord and Master Christ, whom they all so gloriously taught and
> confessed: that He has received a name above all names from the
> Father, who made Him Lord and Christ and set Him on His holy
> Mt. Zion and gave Him the nations for an inheritance and the world
> for a possession [cf. Phil. 2:9, Acts 2:36, Ps. 2:6, 8].[40]

Katharina Schütz Zell was a devout Christian reformer, a typical
Protestant of the first generation. Having been released from the
anxious hell of trying to earn her own reassurance of salvation, KSZ
spent the rest of her life striving to be a good "fisher," one who tries
to bring others into the net of Christ's redemption and love. KSZ knew
what she believed and what that faith required of her, and she devoted
her life to witnessing to her faith and practicing its love. KSZ was not
always a comfortable person, any more than most of her colleagues
among the reformers were comfortable people. She was a person of faith
and compassion, of strength and outspoken honesty, of humor, intel-
ligence, and a deep, biblically formed religious devotion.

40. *Ein Brieff,* F3v-F4r. See 1553 letter, 10r.

6. The Role of History in the Theological Enterprise

James Hennesey, S.J.

For many ways of doing theology under Christian auspices, historical study is of no importance, or very little importance. It is peripheral, decorative, useful when it helps establish a position, but easily discarded when it proves inconvenient. Richard Price put it this way:

> Does church history matter? Is the study of Christianity in the early centuries more than an antiquarian pursuit? The answer given by the theologians is a verbal "yes" that thinly veils a mental "no."[1]

Theologians both conservative and liberal are one in their manipulation of history for pragmatic purposes, differing only slightly in their method. History is for most at best a source of "proof texts" or "exempla." The liberal may use the past to chip away at some presently existing norm; the conservative to back a position already held. Neither is genuinely interested in history and its inductive method. In theory this is a more serious situation for those whose framework of understanding Christianity is "Catholic" than it is for those whose understanding has been shaped by a "Protestant" background. Owen Chadwick pointed this out in his *Catholicism in History,* discussing the

---

1. Richard Price, review of W. H. C. Frend, *The Rise of Christianity,* in *The Tablet* (London), 15 December 1984, 1267.

"Catholic" commitment to using tradition, along with scripture, to uncover God's self-revelation. "Commitment to tradition," Chadwick wrote, "was also a commitment to history, and a main reason why the study of history was inescapable in Catholic teaching."[2]

The importance given to "tradition" by those with a "Catholic" approach to Christianity, and particularly by Roman Catholics, is well known.[3] Reacting to the second Vatican Council's document on divine revelation, the Scots theologian J. K. S. Reid has pointed to its treatment of tradition as "the broadest and deepest gulf that separates the Reformed churches from the Roman."[4] Roman Catholicism has insisted officially on involving "tradition" in explaining how we meet the self-revelation of God. Reid saw that and objected; Chadwick, an Anglican, saw it and approved. But when we move from theory to practice, the plain fact is that church history, where presumably one to some degree at least finds the tradition unfolding, has achieved in modern times a role in the Roman Catholic theological enterprise scarcely different from, and sometimes inferior to, the role it has in Protestant circles.

The reasons for this vary. The "presentists," for whom the past is irrelevant, made their voice heard in Protestantism by the turn of the century. Typical was Episcopal Bishop Charles D. Williams of Michigan:

> The only question that concerns us today is, what is the character of the stream that reaches us . . . ? Is the water of life today as it was of old? Can it quench the thirst of our souls? Can it invigorate our moral and ethical life? If it can do these things, we will accept

2. Owen Chadwick, *Catholicism in History* (Cambridge: Cambridge University Press, 1978), quoted in a review by John Tracy Ellis, *America,* 4 November 1978, 315.

3. See, for example, the claim of Norman Tanner, that his edition of *Decrees of the Ecumenical Councils* "for Christians, at least for Roman Catholics . . . may be regarded as the most authoritative work in the world after the Bible." *Decrees of the Ecumenical Councils: I: Nicaea I to Lateran V; II: Trent to Vatican II* (London & Washington, DC: Sheed & Ward, Georgetown University Press, 1990), vii.

4. Reid is quoted by Joseph Ratzinger, "The Transmission of Divine Revelation," ch. 2 in Herbert Vorgrimler, ed., *Commentary on the Documents of Vatican II,* vol. 3 (New York: Herder & Herder, 1969), 188.

it as valid for today. If it cannot, we must reject it, no matter how authentic its origin or traditions.[5]

Undoubtedly, the rejection of history and its part in Christian tradition was made easier by echoes of "Bible alone" in those of Protestant heritage, but as John O'Malley recently suggested, Martin Luther was opposed not so much to the notion of tradition in Christian understanding as to the philosophers' role in medieval Catholicism.[6] Speaking of the situation up until the end of the eighteenth century, Bernard Reardon of the University of Newcastle has reminded us that

> in its basic orthodoxy, an inheritance from Christian antiquity which in the main it never questioned, Reformation Protestantism was at one with Catholicism. Indeed the reformers themselves were unmistakable products of the Middle Ages and shared most of their opponents' presuppositions.

Reardon's conclusion was that

> It is no exaggeration to say . . . that despite the great theological cleavage of the sixteenth century and the bitter theological controversies to which it gave rise, the fundamental unity of Christian thought in the west continued unimpaired until the latter part of the eighteenth century.[7]

By then, of course, new intellectual forces that were shaping the western world came into play, and "Catholic" and "Protestant" approaches took divergent paths.

In the nineteenth century, when science, technology, and social revolution, together with the philosophical revolution sparked by Kant, Hegel, and others, challenged previously accepted Christian values, the post-Reformation traditions took divergent paths. Theology had

5. Herbert W. Schneider, *Religion in 20th Century America* (Cambridge: Harvard University Press, 1952), 132.

6. John W. O'Malley, "Developments, Reforms, and Two Great Reformations: Towards a Historical Assessment of Vatican II," *Theological Studies* 44 (1983): 373-406.

7. Bernard M. G. Reardon, ed., *Religious Thought in the Nineteenth Century* (Cambridge: Cambridge University Press, 1966), 3.

to assimilate, or assimilate to, the vastly changed world situation or, alternatively, in Reardon's words, "fall back on the stronghold of an absolute authority." Mainline Protestant thinkers moved in the first direction; fundamentalists clung to the old verities. Among Roman Catholics, the process was reversed.[8] The Roman center, as Irish theologian Gabriel Daly has put it, responded to the nineteenth-century ideological revolution by rejecting historical imagination and procedures in favor of a reawakened essentialist metaphysics that led to that substantialist interpretation of history described by Robin Collingwood in *The Idea of History*.[9] Deductive arguments from the "nature" of this or that phenomenon accompanied and supported dogmatic pronouncements, in an approach analyzed by Lord Acton:

> It made the teaching of the Church the sole foundation and test of certain knowledge, a criterion alike of the records of history and of the arguments of unbelief. It recognized no means of ascertaining the truth of facts, or the authenticity of documents, sufficiently trustworthy to interfere with theological opinions. It supposed the part of malice and ignorance to be so large, and the powers of unaided reason so minute, that ecclesiastical authority could be the only guide, even in matters foreign to its immediate domain — the next place given to the presumptive authority of the more probable opinion. . . . Hence it was held impossible to verify the facts of religious history, or to argue from the monuments of tradition.[10]

History's role was summed up by Henry Edward Manning, Anglican archdeacon become Roman cardinal:

> The Church indeed has a history. Its course and its act have been recorded by human hands. It has its annals, like the empire of Rome or of Britain. But its history is no more than footprints in time, which record indeed, but cause nothing and create nothing.[11]

8. Reardon, 1-3.

9. R. B. Collingwood, *The Idea of History* (Oxford/New York: Oxford University Press, 1956), 42-45.

10. John Acton, "Ultramontanism," *Essays on Church and State by Lord Acton*, ed. Douglas Woodruff (London: Hollis & Carter, 1952), 49.

11. Henry Edward Manning, "The Vatican Council and Its Definitions" (Pastoral Letter to the Clergy; London, 1870), 123.

Deprived of the assistance of inductive historical study, Roman Catholicism turned instead to a method of explicitation by logical inference of what was implicit in an immutable transhistorical revelation. Owen Chadwick has traced the larger story of these theologians, many of them my own Jesuit brethren, in his book, *From Bossuet to Newman*.[12] Howland Sanks has supplemented Chadwick's work with a study of the nineteenth-century Jesuits at the Gregorian University in Rome and showed how at their apogee with Louis Billot (1846-1931), "the prince of theologians," the idea of "tradition" became linked with the voice of living authority in the church.[13] Pope Pius IX's impatient *bon mot* in 1870 when an Italian cardinal told him that the doctrine of papal infallibility could not be found in the tradition, "Tradition? I am tradition!" reflected the new reality, and a theology of papal *magisterium* developed to support that reality.[14]

Tracing the story of the concept "ordinary magisterium," John Boyle has shown that "the exercise of the papal teaching authority became more frequent and more insistent." Noting that the first use of the term "ordinary magisterium" in a papal document occurred only in 1863, Boyle pointed to consequent repeated assertions of teaching authority of both pope and papal departments, especially at the expense of theologians.[15] It was all part of the ultramontane movement in Roman Catholicism, which also included increasing governmental centralization in the church and the launching in 1879 of the essentialist Thomistic revival in philosophy.[16] It was a context in which "sound and scholarly appeals to history were uncatholic . . . historical inquiries forms of private judgment . . . and we must receive our history of the primitive church from the infallible teaching of the

12. Owen Chadwick, *From Bossuet to Newman: The Idea of Doctrinal Development* (Cambridge: Cambridge University Press, 1957).

13. T. Howland Sanks, *Authority in the Church: A Study in Changing Paradigms* (Missoula: Scholars Press, 1974), 80 (for Billot's position).

14. Michele Maccarrone, *II Concilio Vaticano I e il "Giornale" di Mons. Arrigoni*, vol. 1 (Pauda: Antenore, 1966), 428-29 n. 4.

15. John P. Boyle, "The Ordinary Magisterium: Towards a History of the Concept," *The Heythrop Journal* 20 (1979): 381.

16. James Hennesey, "Leo XIII's Thomistic Revival: A Political and Philosophical Event," *The Journal of Religion* 58 (1978): 185-97; James Hennesey, "Leo XIII: Intellectualizing the Combat with Modernity," *U.S. Catholic Historian* 7 (1988): 393-400.

present church."[17] The eminent church historian Hubert Jedin made a frightening assertion of this position when he wrote, "'[T]radition' is the living, teaching office of the church, which authoritatively interprets and complements scripture."[18] That is not Catholic teaching as stated by Vatican II, which carefully distinguished what is interpreted (tradition) from its interpreter (the teaching authority).[19]

The ultramontane approach was further strengthened by the growth and refinement of the canon law. Stephen Kuttner, perhaps the most prominent historian of canon law in the United States, had long since seen as the accomplishment of the medieval canonists that they brought harmony out of dissonance by "indulging in a sublime disregard of history" in shaping their discipline and, incidentally, in shaping official church structure for centuries to come.[20] The great French Dominican historian and theologian, Yves Congar, put that in perspective when he wrote of the fabrications on which much of the medieval canon law was based that they "not only ruined the chances of historical development, [but also] gave credence to the notion that all the determinations of the church's life flowed from the papacy as their source."[21]

The ultramontane spirit was brought to a fine legal point in the production (1904-19) of the first-ever Code of Canon Law, set in train by Pope Pius X (1903-14).[22] Papacy and church were seen in juridical terms, exercising authority that was more legalistic than it was spiritual or charismatic.

History in these circumstances was reduced to providing proof texts or exempla, adduced selectively in support of conclusions already

17. This was Owen Chadwick's description of the attitude he found in the very ultramontane nineteenth-century American essayist, Orestes Brownson. (Chadwick, *From Bossuet to Newman,* 171-72).

18. Hubert Jedin, "The Second Vatican Council," in *History of the Church,* ed. Hubert Jedin, vol. 10 (New York: Crossroads, 1981), 141.

19. Walter M. Abbott, ed., *Documents of Vatican II* (New York: Herder & Herder, 1966), ch. 2, "The Transmission of Divine Revelation," 114-18.

20. Stephen Kuttner, *Harmony from Dissonance: An Interpretation of Medieval Canon Law* (Latrobe: St. Vincent's Archabbey Press, 1960), 35.

21. Yves Congar, *L'Église de saint Augustin a l'époque moderne* (Paris: Éditions de Cerf, 1970), 63.

22. Pierre Fernessole, *Pie X: Essai historique,* vol. 2 (Paris: P. Lethiellieux, 1953), 151-58.

arrived at by other means. A contemporary American bishop indicated its place when he explained how to give a talk on a "Catholic" topic:

> Take a clear Catholic position on just about anything, develop it with philosophical precision, and illustrate the development with citations from the fathers, the classic theologians, and the encyclicals of the popes.[23]

A casual reference in a 1986 working document prepared for the U.S. Catholic Bishops' Committee on the Laity reinforces the evidence that history has come on hard times. The document proposes that conclusions drawn by the committee be critiqued from the standpoint of scripture, the documents of church councils, and the Code of Canon Law, all taken together as representing "universal church tradition."[24] Scripture is, of course, basic to church tradition, and conciliar documents and legal codes have their role to play, but they hardly make up "universal church tradition." The second Vatican Council, in its constitution on divine revelation, speaks of tradition as "the teaching, life and worship" of the church, the Christian community down the ages.[25] The contemporary Roman Catholic church historian sees him/herself as contributing to tradition's elucidation by the study of those areas, which are far broader in scope than either the bishop or the working document allowed. It is important to stress the need to study the life of the church, the actual lived experience of the Christian community. This includes not only structures, but faith-life, and should be both descriptive and scientifically analyzed with the help of social-science tools. Not to be neglected is discovery of authentic church tradition in the individual and corporate prayer-life of members of the community. Modern Roman Catholic historians do not take the approach critiqued by John Noonan when he described the 1930 papal encyclical, *Casti Connubii:*

> As a distillation of past doctrinal statements, the encyclical was a masterpiece. At the same time, its composers were indifferent to the

---

23. Edward M. Egan, "Trends in American Spirituality," *Origins* 16 (30 October 1986): 35.

24. National Council of Catholic Bishops Committee on the Laity, memorandum for August 1986 Working Convocation, in possession of author.

25. Abbott, 116.

historical contexts from which their citations came and uninterested in the environmental changes which differentiated the present context. The encyclical was a synthesis; it was not history.[26]

Nineteenth-century Roman Catholics had another approach, or rather, several different approaches. An early example is found in the 1784 "Address to the Roman Catholics of the United States of America," a response to Charles Wharton's strictures on Roman Catholicism penned by his cousin John Carroll (1736-1815), later the first Roman Catholic bishop in the United States. Taking up each point raised by Wharton, Carroll argued from the scriptures, the church fathers, later theologians both Protestant and Catholic, and the life and practice of Christian people. The "Address," which made little or no appeal to papal authority, was a classic exercise in inductive, historical theology. In their different ways the Englishman John Henry Newman (1801-1890) and the southwest Germans of the Tübingen school kept alive ideas of growth, development, and change as the stuff of history, as they sought to reconcile them with continuity.[27] These tendencies, together with the more strictly historico-critical work of authors like the French expert on the early church Louis Duchesne (1843-1922), were put on hold during the turn-of-the-century modernist/integrist crisis, but came to fruition with the adoption of a historico-biblical approach in the second Vatican Council (1962-64).[28]

H. Richard Niebuhr caught very well the Roman church that was the product of the mainline developments discussed earlier. As he painted the picture, Protestantism emerged from the nineteenth century drawn to the dynamic, while the Roman Catholic had a sense

26. John Noonan, Jr., *Contraception: A Study of Its Treatment by the Catholic Theologians and Canonists* (Cambridge: Harvard University Press, 1966), 427.

27. John Carroll, "Address to the Roman Catholics of the United States of America," *The John Carroll Papers,* vol. 1, ed. Thomas O'Brien Hanley (Notre Dame: University of Notre Dame Press, 1976), 82-144. Wharton, like Carroll a former Jesuit, became an Episcopal clergyman in the United States.

28. For a recent appreciation of Duchesne, see Glenn F. Chesnut, "A Century of Patristic Studies," in *A Century of Church History: The Legacy of Philip Schaff,* ed. Henry W. Bowden (Carbondale/Edwardsville: Southern Illinois University Press, 1988), 48-51.

of being part of an established order of things, member of an enduring and fundamentally unchanging church, recipient of a truth once and for all revealed, believer in a well-defined and articulated "true religion," subject of constant and known laws, follower of leaders who stand in an unchanging office and succession.

To the Protestant, on the other hand, Neibuhr wrote,

Life seemed a pilgrim's progress, of encounters between God and man to be re-enacted in every generation, through unpredictable contingencies and crises toward the destination beyond life and death where all the trumpets blow.[29]

The picture is not now so clear-cut, if indeed it ever was. In a document prepared for the international bishops' synod held in Rome in 1987, the Roman Catholic bishops of England and Wales pictured a church that was not "as an army marching in formation, but more like a group of travellers in a desert." Using imagery drawn from the second Vatican Council, the bishops emphasized the notion of a "pilgrim people," a community in which the laity as well as church professionals were expected to take proper initiatives and shoulder their responsibilities.[30]

Something had happened to the church of Cardinal Alfredo Ottaviani, the redoubtable conservative leader of Vatican II days, whose coat-of-arms bore the proud motto, "Semper Idem," "Always the Same." Something had happened to the test of orthodoxy laid down by the fifth-century stalwart Vincent of Lerins when he wrote that "what is Catholic is that which has been believed everywhere, always and by all." There had been a revolution in thinking, an acceptance of historicization. Joseph Ratzinger, now head of the Roman Congregation for the doctrine of the faith and chief watchdog of orthodoxy for the Holy See, commented of Vincent's "static *semper*," that it "no longer seems the right way of expressing the nature

29. H. Richard Niebuhr, "The Protestant Movement and Democracy in the United States," in *The Shaping of American Religion*, ed. James W. Smith and A. Leland Jamison (Princeton: Princeton University Press, 1961), 22-23.

30. "Statement of the Roman Catholic Bishops of England and Wales," *The Tablet* (London), 24 May 1986, 249.

of historical identity and continuity." We must acknowledge, he wrote, "the historicity of a church which is still under way and will become itself only when the ways of time have been travelled."[31]

An articulate and conservative theologian, Bishop Walter Kasper, summed it up:

> We are experiencing a radical historicization of all reality. Everything is involved in upheaval and change. Little or nothing remains firm and constant. What were once regarded as eternal truths and binding traditions now carry little or no weight.

It is for him an experience of "metamorphoses and developments in the church's pattern of faith," taking place "not only in accordance with the laws of organic growth," but proceeding "by leaps and bounds, shifts, anticipations and retardations."[32]

American historian John W. O'Malley has written of the need to recognize "discontinuity" in the church's history;[33] Yves Congar pointed some years back to two ways of understanding church history as a branch of theology: (1) seeing in it development, a progressive revelation of what had heretofore been implicit; and (2) seeing through history "a series of formulations of the one content of faith diversifying and finding different expression in different cultural contexts."[34] In Robin Collingwood's phrase, we have become "historically conscious," able to think of theological formulations in terms of their culture-bound and historically contingent character, interpreting previous traditions in terms of present self-understanding. History is no longer, in Collingwood's words, "frozen solid"; it is dynamic.[35]

This new Catholic approach fits well with studies done on "the tradition and traditions" in Faith and Order conferences at Edinburgh in 1937 and Montreal in 1963. At Edinburgh, "the Tradition" was

31. Joseph Ratzinger, "The Ecclesiology of the Second Vatican Council," *Communio* 13 (1986): 249.

32. Walter Kasper, "Are Church and Theology Subject to Historical Law?" *The Crisis of Change* (Chicago: Argus, 1969), 7, 9.

33. John W. O'Malley, "Reform, Historical Consciousness, and Vatican II's Aggiornamento," *Theological Studies* 32 (1971): 591-601.

34. Yves Congar, "Church History as a Branch of Theology," *Concilium* 57 (1970): 87.

35. Collingwood, 43.

spoken of as "the living stream of the church's life" and as the "ongoing life of the church." It was distinguished from "traditions," which are diverse formulations, and particularly confessional approaches. Montreal's final report stated, "By *the Tradition* is meant the gospel itself, transmitted from generation to generation in and by the church, Christ himself present in the church."[36] By the way they place emphases, Protestant and Catholic understandings of the respective roles of scripture and tradition still stand apart, but not nearly so much as they did in the heat of sixteenth-century controversies.

For the contemporary Roman Catholic historian, "tradition" is understood to be a sense arising from and discerned in the historical life of the church. It is to be found, Joseph Ratzinger says, "not only in the explicitly traditional statements of church doctrine, but in the unstated, and often unstatable, elements of the whole service of the worship of God and the life of the church."[37] There is good hope that common ground can be found with Protestant historians of similar views. The Eastern Orthodox, about whom nothing has been said, have a deep sense of tradition, but might not find themselves comfortable with some of the approaches described; certainly a goodly number of fundamentalists, if with different nuances, on both sides of the Reformation divide would be equally uneasy. Nevertheless, a sea change has taken place on the Roman side.

The classicist, or substantialist, mind-set that came into sharp focus during the ultramontane years of the nineteenth and early twentieth centuries allowed only for external, accidental changes as the church passed through time. That mind-set produced an image of the church that emphasized order and unchangeableness. It was the church of Vincent of Lerins, whose obituary Joseph Ratzinger has written. There was no room or reason for historical study. "Tradition" was conceived of as an arcane, ill-defined treasure trove of propositional statements waiting the providential moment for enunication.

Two factors changed all that. One was the emergence of the historico-critical method, applied not only to the scriptures, but to the

36. *A History of the Ecumenical Movement,* vol. 2, *The Ecumenical Advance,* ed. Harold E. Fey (Philadelphia: Westminster Press, 1967-70), 159-61 (quotation, 160).
37. Ratzinger, *Commentary on the Documents of Vatican II,* vol. 3, 184.

memories and documents of the past. The other was the realization, profound and genuine, of the pervasiveness and consequences of change. The historian's task, whatever relative importance he/she attaches to tradition and traditions, is to distinguish the one from the other. Like the biblical exegete, the historian is not a solo actor, but a partner, in the complex process of "doing theology." Historians offer the results of their historico-critical research, they testify to the pervasiveness of change, but they understand, as Robert Taft has put it, that the results of their investigations are for theologians instructive, never normative.[38] A historian is not necessarily a historicist. We put our study at the service of the wider congress of the theologians and students of religion. It is a cooperative venture in which no one should be a monologuist.

38. Robert Taft, "The Frequency of the Eucharist throughout History," *Concilium* 152 (1982): 13-24.

III. CONCLUSION AND BIBLIOGRAPHIC ESSAY

7. Reflections on an Ecumenical-Historical Experiment

Thomas Finger

The fourteen principles of ecumenical historiography them-selves have a history; or, better said, they have emerged from several histories, from ongoing discussions in several overlapping domains. In their preface, Charles Brockwell and Timothy Wengert discuss the principles' connections with the current discipline of church history (connections quite apparent in Fred Norris's essay on Arianism). This conclusion begins by briefly tracing their roots in the ecumenical movement. It will then address the issues raised in the preceding essays, grouping them according to two frequently appearing themes: "The Normative and the Descriptive" (Section II) and "Globality and Difference" (Section IV), intersected by comments on "Cooperative Method" (Section III).

I. The Ecumenical Background

In the opinion of many, the worldwide ecumenical movement has entered a period of uncertainty, perhaps even pessimism. According to Konrad Raiser, recently appointed General Secretary of the W.C.C., ecumenicism was increasingly energized during the 1950s and '60s by a crystallizing vision of "Christocentric Universalism." Ecumenists, that is, became ever more convinced that the Spirit was not only drawing churches together on the basis of their common confession of Jesus Christ as "God and Savior," but drawing humankind in all nations toward cooperative harmony as well. Consequently, following the 1968 Uppsala Assembly, the Faith and Order Commission launched a study on "The Unity of the Church and the Unity of Humankind," initially regarding the two as parallel, complementary processes.[1] As Günther Gassmann has shown, these movements toward universalism seemed to require establishment of "a 'genuinely universal council' that could speak for all Christians." To bring about the sacramental and confessional unity prerequisite for such a council, Faith and Order subsequently initiated studies on *Baptism, Eucharist and Ministry* (1972) and *Confessing the Apostolic Faith Today* (1981).

Yet the more it has striven toward unity, the more diversity the ecumenical movement has encountered. As additional non-Western churches became involved, and as marginalized groups within all churches began finding their voices, they frequently raised issues that differed from and conflicted with traditional ecumenical agenda. Moreover, socio-historical processes during the 1970s and '80s increasingly spawned divisions between north and south, rich and poor, humankind and its environment, and among nations and religions. Against this background, efforts at sacramental, structural, and confessional church unity began appearing to many as bureaucratic concerns of ecclesiastical specialists. According to Raiser, at least, many in the ecumenical movement have reached a point of confusion over all this diversity, and enthusiasm for pursuing its universal goals has waned.[2]

The fourteen principles emerged from an encounter with this diversity within the National Council of the Churches of Christ, U.S.A. Much of the impetus was provided by Jeffrey Gros, its director of Faith and Order from 1981 to 1991. Gros deliberately sought participation by groups normally outside NCCC and WCC circles. During his tenure, consultations were held on such themes as *Black Witness to the Apostolic Faith*[3] and "The Apostolic Character of the Church's Peace

1. Konrad Raiser, *Ecumenism in Transition* (Geneva: WCC Publications, 1991), 33-53.
2. Raiser, 1-30, 54-78.
3. David Shannon and Gayraud Wilmore, eds. (Grand Rapids: Eerdmans, 1987).

Witness,"[4] while several dialogues were initiated with Pentecostals.[5] As NCCC Faith and Order, in harmony with the WCC, undertook the *Confessing the Apostolic Faith Today* study during its 1982-84 "triennium," this new diversity began making itself felt. The study was to take the Nicene-Constantinopolitan Creed as its basis. After repeated failures to get off the ground, the basic reason for the lack of success emerged: many American churches do not really use this Creed.

During the 1985-87 triennium, it proved necessary to begin at a more fundamental level. Rather than assuming the normativity of the Creed (and rather than challenging or denying it), representatives of the varied traditions were asked, "Simply tell us how 'confessing,' 'apostolicity,' and 'faith' would be understood in your communion." Sharing of the differing perspectives revealed that while some understood these terms credally, others interpreted them chiefly in, say, ethical or praxeological ways. What resulted was not really disagreement over the Creed's content, but awareness of a variety of ways of being Christian. Though the common core of such an "apostolicity" was difficult to define, participants generally emerged more convinced about the sincerity of other groups' intentions to be apostolic.[6]

The fourteen principles arose from an extension of the experiences and methodology discovered in this study to history. Once again, Jeff Gros took the lead. He proposed that if churches "are to find paths to reconciliation in Jesus Christ, we must learn to tell a common story."[7] Gros affirmed that a common "global history of the Church and an account of the history of doctrine" would be useful. Yet he called chiefly for a "process by which common accounts can be written of key Church-dividing moments, so that they might heal the memories of the past and challenge Christians to find a common identity in which their diversity can be celebrated."[8] Gros stressed the importance

---

4. See Jeffrey Gros, "Exploring the Apostolic Faith: The Peace Churches' Contribution," *Ecumenical Trends* 19, no. 6 (June 1990): 92-94.

5. See Jeffrey Gros, "Confessing the Apostolic Faith from the Perspective of the Pentecostal Churches," *Pneuma* 9, no. 1 (Spring 1987): 5-16.

6. For an account of this process, see Thaddeus Horgan, ed., *Apostolic Faith in America* (Grand Rapids: Eerdmans, 1988).

7. Jeffrey Gros, "Interpretation, History and the Ecumenical Movement," *Ecumenical Trends* 16, no. 7 (July/August 1987): 117.

8. Gros, "Interpretation," 117.

of doing this work "corporately," in "the Faith and Order style," rather than in the individualistic and competitive manner he found characteristic of academia.[9]

While seven of the eight scholars who originally responded to this proposal lauded many of its features,[10] some pointed out that it involved inherent tensions. Melanie May (Church of the Brethren) noted that it sought to reach commonality, paradoxically, by "multiplication of sources, experiences, and perspectives." Yet, "to take context seriously," she stressed, "is to take difference seriously."[11] Timothy George (Southern Baptist) insisted that "we cannot paper over the real theological, liturgical and church political differences."[12] For some, this historical diversity posed serious obstacles. Mark Noll, representing an evangelicalism largely outside the NCCC, felt that "ecumenism . . . requires historical amnesia, rather than historical reconstruction,"[13] while Stanley Harakas (Greek Orthodox) warned that the historical method itself could dissolve all transcendent, unifying truth "in a sea of contextualism."[14] Yet others, like May, found historiography's emphasis on context and difference a "challenge . . . to conceive unity not in terms of conformity or constraint, but with regard to difference . . . to cultivate bonds of unity that celebrate rather than condemn difference."[15] Respondents generally welcomed Gros's call for a cooperative methodology. However, Max Stackhouse (United Church of Christ), cautioned that collaborative efforts can be as ideological as individual ones.[16]

9. Gros, "Interpretation," 119.

10. Timothy Smith (Church of the Nazarene) regarded Gros's project as a rewriting of history "to serve a particular cause . . . to make history purposeful propaganda" (Gros, "Interpretation," 133). The responses of Roberta Bondi (at 122-23) and George Tavard (at 128-30), United Methodist and Roman Catholic, were more positive.

11. Gros, "Interpretation," 130; Smith predicted that the Latin America CEHILA Project, which Gros lauded, would expand, not narrow, the range of conflicting interpretations (at 133).

12. Gros, "Interpretation," 132.

13. Gros, "Interpretation," 132.

14. Gros, "Interpretation," 125; Max Stackhouse (United Church of Christ) cautioned that "current fascination with the 'contextual' nature of Christian history" could overlook "how much trans-contextual claims about God's truth and justice have shaped contexts" (at 128).

15. Gros, "Interpretation," 131.

16. Gros, "Interpretation," 127.

Stimulated by Gros's proposal, Faith and Order established an "Apostolic Faith History Study" during its next quadrennium (1988-91). Many of us present at its first sessions, however, can scarcely recall occasions where hopes for ecumenical understanding seemed more frustrated. Differences in perspective, current interests, and expertise seemed to preclude even minimal clarity as to what we were about. Surprisingly, though, a common focus emerged when we adapted a method from earlier Apostolic Faith studies. Whereas those participants had been asked, "Simply tell us how 'apostolicity,' say, would be understood in your communion," current participants were requested to describe straightforwardly how a standard church history — Williston Walker's *A History of the Christian Church*[17] — would look from their denomination's perspective. Despite differences in these evaluations, certain commonalities appeared. It was generally agreed, for instance, that Walker's treatment was overly Protestant, Western, institutional, white, and masculine. By simply considering a common subject, and by freely expressing perspectival responses without pressure for premature conformity, enough common ground, or at least consensus as to what some major issues were, had emerged to spark deeper discussion about similarities and differences in interpreting history.

In addition to producing the fourteen principles, the Apostolic Faith–History study organized consultations on two "key church-dividing moments" highlighted by Gros. A conference on the fourth century explored the interplay among social, political, ecclesiastical, and theological elements in the emergence of Constantine and the Creed. Churches that have viewed these developments quite positively and those that have assessed them quite negatively participated. While some differences remained, some common ground also emerged. Participants gained appreciation of why others perceive things as they do, and acknowledged that "[e]ven in our disagreements, we experienced the capacity of the Creed to unify us by directing our attention to the faith we share."[18] Contributions to a second consultation, on American-born churches (originating in the nineteenth century), came almost entirely from communions outside the NCCC — an event per-

---

17. 4th ed., rev. R. Norris, D. Lotz, and R. Handy (New York: Charles Scribners' Sons, 1985).

18. Mark Heim, ed., *From Faith to Creed* (Grand Rapids: Eerdmans, 1991).

haps unique in its history.[19] This consultation underlined a conclusion of the earlier Apostolic Faith studies: though these churches may have produced fragmenting effects, they arose from sincere efforts to affirm, rather than deny, a genuine "apostolicity."[20]

The fourteen principles, then, did not emerge in a vacuum. They constitute an attempt not to *prescribe* how church history should be written, but to *describe* procedures beginning to be utilized in various academic and ecumenical circles. Their formulators intend them as one voice in an ongoing dialogue — as hypotheses, even as questions asking, "Is this the way it is being/should be done?" — whose usefulness can be determined only by answers gained through application to concrete situations. The essays in this volume, then, represent the first such answers. In light of them, the hypotheses may require modification. And should such modification inspire further research, in turn necessitating further alteration, these principles will be fulfilling their basic purpose.

This conclusion comprises one attempt to ascertain "What have we learned so far? Where have the principles proved most illuminating? Where might they require revision?" Since Richard Norris has already taken us serially through the principles, clearly exhibiting their overlapping character, I will group my remarks according to the issues mentioned above. While I will represent the entire study group as well as I can, I must acknowledge two limitations. First, the group as a whole could discuss only two essays (Hennesey's and McKee's). Second, I, like everyone else, come with my own perspective. Academically, I am not primarily a historian but a theologian. Denominationally, I represent a communion traditionally outside the NCCC and WCC, the Mennonites. Yet the inclusion of such a commentator accords well with the principles' orientation. In any case, while refraining from claims to "complete objectivity," I will strive for "fair-minded empathy" (Principle 14).

19. Traditions from which papers were presented were as follows: Christian Methodist Episcopal, Church of God in Christ, Church of the Nazarene, Restorationist (Disciples), and Seventh Day Adventist.
20. See Horgan.

II. The Normative and the Descriptive

Whenever new areas or methods of historical research are proposed, certain general questions arise about their nature and justification. Today, when claims to objectivity are highly suspect, supporters — and especially critics — of such proposals inevitably seek to unearth the values and presuppositions involved, whether explicit or implicit. To the question of what assumptions, beliefs, and commitments may underlie the scope and procedures of the fourteen principles I apply the term "normative."

In chapter 3 Günther Gassmann observes that the principles employ terms like "Christian history," "ecumenical history," and "church history" somewhat interchangeably, while in chapter 2 Richard Norris finds that such looseness "raises a question about the subject matter of this . . . enterprise." Norris feels that the term "church" would "require theological definition." Yet he supposes that the principles intend a more phenomenological, descriptive approach, as expressed by the phrase "the story of all who call themselves Christians" (Principle 1). Norris correctly senses that the study group initially sought to steer away from theological definitions.[21] Yet the principles do contain definitions and cite warrants that many would call theological. According to the explication of Principle 1, for instance, ecumenical historiography "recognizes church wherever" Jesus is confessed "as 'Lord and God' (John 20:28), 'the Christ, the Son of the Living God' (Matt. 16:16)" — phrases that recall the WCC's confession. The Scripture citations that accompany this and many other principles are apparently invoked not, surely, as conclusive proof texts, but as indications of the kind of biblical-theological grounding that could be provided.

Yet, however explicitly or implicitly normative theological criteria may appear in the principles, they do play important roles in two of the essays designed to employ them. Gassmann's critical principle of "globality," which he adds to the fourteen, is one of those "prescriptive theories, concepts, ideals, and goals that are intended to shape ecumenical history and that . . . provide the writing of Christian history with intrinsic criteria for positive and critical evaluation."

21. See Norris's comments on Principle 5 on pp. 29-30 above.

Globality can be further interpreted with the help of the "theological criterion" of "catholicity." Gassmann then uses the resulting fifteen principles chiefly to distinguish this normative global thrust from other dimensions of "Christian history" more broadly and more phenomenologically understood.

Fred Norris commences his study of Arianism by bracketing the traditional theological verdict upon it. Like Elsie McKee, he employs Principles 5 and 6 in some detail, constructing quite a different picture of Arianism, informed by its hymns and popular practices. Nonetheless, Norris doubts that use of the principles "can avoid the questions of heresy and orthodoxy" (p. 68 above). This is largely because current, more favorable appraisals of Arianism, as well as current critiques of it, both "work from stated commitments about what modern Christianity is and should be." In other words, the theological issues that sparked the Arian controversy are still alive and clearly shape the "values and commitments" employed in studying it.

Fred Norris himself finds the historic orthodox claim, that "the creed reflects a wider base in both scripture and tradition than what is found among the Arian leaders," most convincing. This claim, he maintains, forms part of the received *consensus fidelium* that helps define what the church is today, and that any ecumenical historiography must take seriously. Nevertheless, Norris's study does not simply ratify the Nicene-Constantinopolitan decision. His efforts at sympathetic portrayal uncover many valid Christian concerns operative in Arianism, however one may judge its theological formulations. His study reminds us who seek for ecumenical understanding today "how slowly consensus is built, how cruelly ancient labels can be applied to contemporary Christians, and how often remarkably faithful people seem to be on the other side."

If theological warrants and norms are occasionally implied in the principles, and if two essays designed to employ them make explicit use of such, is the attempt to define their scope descriptively, as "all who call themselves Christians," misguided? If "Christian" or "church," say, lack unambiguous definition, have the principles, in violation of their own number 14, grossly failed to clarify their own presuppositions? From my vantage point, not really. Not, at least, when the principles are viewed within the process from which they arose. For church historical study, as James Hennesey shows, has often been guided by normative theological definitions. Yet such commitments have often hindered it from discovering the unexpected and unique. They have often reduced it "to providing proof texts, or *exempla,* adduced selectively in support of conclusions already arrived at by other means."

The ecumenical movement in general, and the Apostolic Faith studies in particular, have experienced the same thing. Too often, presupposed definitions of "Christian" or "church" have hindered one communion from hearing another. But when such definitions are bracketed, and when the parties are simply invited to tell, descriptively, how things look from their standpoint, surprising features of being Christian or church come to the fore. Often, of course, those prior definitions would not have directly contradicted the new insights; yet they can promote a mind-set that watches so carefully for certain features that it is insufficiently open to the unexpected. They can foster an attitude that expects the truly Christian to emerge only by " 'laws of organic growth' " and not also " 'by leaps and bounds, shifts, anticipations and retardations.' "[22]

The Apostolic Faith studies, then, have borne fruit when normative limits on what counts as "church" or "Christian" have been provisionally suspended and attention has turned toward a wider field, that "of all who call themselves Christian." Precisely speaking, however, only the edges of this field have been explored. Investigation has really been expanded only to communions that, while outside NCCC circles, generally affirm its Christocentric confession. While planners for the American-born Churches Consultation wrestled with inviting groups such as Jehovah's Witnesses and Mormons, such were finally not included. And the study group hardly touched on numerous new movements, especially in Latin America and Africa, that blend many features of local religions and Christianity. While ecumenists generally regard such groups as syncretistic cults, most would likely "call themselves Christian."

Yet if this descriptive term is so very broad — one might insist — will it not eventually lead to data so varied, clashing, and confusing that ecumenical historiography will have to arrive at *some* clear normative definitions? At present, this is an open question. Some study

22. Hennesey, quoting Walter Kasper.

group members apparently fear that any precise "limits to diversity" would erect inhospitable, exclusionary walls. Others, like me, feel that any coherent ecumenical project will inevitably move toward such definitions. Still others seem to prefer suspending judgment. But for now the main point, I think, is that the designation of ecumenical historiography's field as "all who call themselves Christian" is best understood not as a permanent definition of its scope, but as a hypothesis about what region can most fruitfully be investigated. It functions, that is, as a guideline, designating what areas are to be explored. Given the dialogical relationship between the principles and specific investigations, it can also be understood as a question — "Is the appropriate field for exploration best described as 'all who call themselves Christian'?" — that only detailed historical work can answer.

The principles can be utilized, then, without taking a definite stance as to whether certain theological norms should guide them or as to precisely what such norms might be. In fact I would argue, paradoxically, that the principles can be employed at present only without fully defining such norms. For even if one believes, as I do, that cooperative investigation presupposes some areas of normative agreement, the exact nature of such agreement is unclear precisely when new territory is being explored. To say it otherwise, the conditions of the possibility of knowledge in any field can be ascertained only by examining the results and procedures actually employed in that field. But while a new field is being established, its results and procedures will be too indefinite to allow any such underlying conditions to be definitively articulated.

III. Cooperative Method

Central to Jeffrey Gros's original proposal, and to the study group's experience, is the process of investigating history together. As a group member, I find its character expressed most clearly in Principles 9-12. Richard Norris's insightful essay, however, devotes only two pages to these four principles, in contrast to the thirteen allotted to the first eight, and says little about the attitudes they commend. While I am unsure of his reasons for this, I wonder whether Norris might be viewing Principles 9-12 largely from the standpoint of "the historian" operating in academia, and may not realize how corporately and ecclesially oriented the whole process is meant to be.

At risk of some overstatement, let me say that these principles regard the partners in ecumenical historiography as, in a certain sense, the various ecclesial traditions themselves. They assume that the historians involved understand themselves not simply as neutral observers, or even as generic Christians, but as those who seek to get "inside" a tradition and to present it empathetically. Often such historians will adhere to the tradition they present. While these may well critique certain of its features, they will be committed to — personally invested in — others. When this kind of involvement is in view, something more than ordinary academic fairness may be needed. Avoiding defensiveness, practicing repentance and forgiveness (Principle 12), and practicing hospitality (Principle 11) may become especially crucial.

One might object that this kind of personal investment renders the project too "subjective." Yet elucidation of traditions "from inside" can open up otherwise inaccessible dimensions, particularly in traditions "whose story has been ignored or suppressed" (Principle 1). For such groups have usually been described and evaluated through their opponents' categories. Depicted in such terms, they often appear heretical or simply nonsensical. But if described "from inside," if allowed to speak for themselves, their experiences and claims often manifest a surprising inner logic and intersect with other traditions at unexpected points. Principle 9 insists that such traditions speak in their own voices, even if these employ other than standard academic or ecclesiastical discourse.

In this process, however, a certain "objectivity," or certain more "objective" reference points, can be attained. For the various spokespersons are envisioned as speaking not simply to themselves, nor to a faceless scholarly audience, but directly to representatives for other traditions. And these representatives, including those from more dominant traditions, are speaking from their own internal standpoints, too. From these positions, all participants usually come across somewhat differently than in standard historical renderings. And if all parties interact hospitably and nondefensively, each tradition can gradually be opened "to critical analysis by others" (Principle 10). Such an atmosphere of give-and-take often enables the various traditions to assess their past experiences and claims from a vantage point of greater critical distance, or objectivity, than would evaluation by usual historical or theological standards.

The principles, then, speak of course to "the historian" seeking to investigate her or his subject matter fairly and empathetically. But they also are intended for spokespersons, as it were, seeking to deal appropriately with data, questions, challenges, and criticisms introduced from other standpoints. They envision ecumenical historiography above all as continuing dialogue, in which other peoples' perceptions, discoveries, reconsiderations, and reinterpretations keep affecting the way one sees the past. The present volume, unfortunately, can embody this process only partially. It might have done so more fully if, for instance, rather than having this writer respond to all the essays, the essayists could have responded to each other, and then responded to each other's responses to them. Yet such an undertaking would have been far more complicated. We must be content with small beginnings.

Of the essays in this volume, Hennesey's makes fullest use of Principles 9-12. If we understand Gassmann to be speaking for the ecumenical "tradition," then he, too, opens it to analysis by others (Principle 10) in a nondefensive way (Principle 12). But Hennesey is clearly speaking out of a specific ecclesial tradition whose shortcomings he does not shrink from exposing. By tracing differing streams within Roman Catholic historiography, and by noting their convergences with and divergences from Protestant efforts, he helps them all find their voices among the communities of faith (Principle 9).[23]

IV. Globality and Difference

We recall that this tension, often expressed as that between unity and diversity, or universality and particularity, is central to the entire ecumenical enterprise. We remember that Gassmann, in fact, proposed "globality" as a fifteenth principle. On the other hand, the great variety

---

23. Fred Norris and Elsie McKee certainly enable particular voices — in fact, ignored or suppressed voices — to speak, but I emphasize Hennesey's essay here because he is more clearly enabling some within his *own* tradition to do so.

of concerns, approaches, and areas of study evident even in the foregoing essays (which makes summarizing them a challenge!) attests to great differences among ecumenical concerns. They bear out Richard Norris's caution that "universality" of outlook (Principles 1-3) can hardly ever refer to "an account of the whole Christian story." They also recall the observation, initially offered in response to Jeff Gros's proposal, that the effort to reach unity by investigating a greater diversity of sources could lead in the opposite direction. Richard Norris echoes this concern, arguing that the value of much recent research into histories of marginalized groups is bound up with its being to some extent centric or "narrow."

Yet Richard Norris goes much further. He regards the intention "to avoid geographic centrism, classism, ethocentrism, sexism, and the cult of personality" (Principle 2) not as a way — even a paradoxical and difficult way — to becoming "global in outlook," but as the replacement of a geographical by a temporal "centrism." To Norris, these aims represent, not genuine aspirations toward globality, but simply "the intellectual agenda of a particular era." This claim is connected with Norris's deepest critique of the principles: that they subordinate the past to the present, that they unduly pressure history to address today's "lively issues" (Principle 7) rather than allowing it to speak in its own voice (pp. 31-36 above). But do the principles inevitably lead in this direction? Here several of the essays can help us.

Fred Norris, we recall, certainly indicated that the issues clustering around Arianism are alive today. But did his study simply foist today's "intellectual agenda" on the past? The answer depends largely on what one thinks that current agenda is. Contemporary academic historiography, with its concern for marginalized voices, would favor a sympathetic reading of Arianism. Yet the ecumenical agenda, which assigns centrality to the Nicene Creed, would favor a more critical appraisal. Which modern agenda might Fred Norris have been following? He treats Arianism sympathetically. Yet he insists that "the victors also deserve a smidgen of fairness" (p. 64 above). He is finally more affirmative of the orthodox side. Yet he evaluates the issues using not modern criteria, but those proposed by Athanasius and Gregory Nazianzen. To be sure, today's "lively issues" influenced what themes Fred Norris selected and how he handled them. Yet it seems difficult to deny that some hitherto unnoticed ancient voices were heard, or to insist that his conclusions were phrased apart from genuine wrestling with their claims and counterclaims.

One might also ask whether Elsie McKee's Katharina Schütz Zell is just the sort of woman that the principles, if they are unduly biased toward contemporary values, might be expected to find. After all, KSZ fulfills several dimensions of today's feminine ideal, from both the academic-historiographical and the ecumenical standpoints. She is an avid student and teacher, expresses herself well, and works as a team with her husband. Yet McKee is quite aware of the dangers of presenting anyone "as a paradigmatic figure," of reducing "a most distinctive person to a type." Moreover, her portrait of Katharina is intended not chiefly to recommend her as an ideal, but to help us "glimpse the reform movement as a movement." And indeed McKee, in my estimation, does bring certain little-noticed features of the Reformation to light.

For one, she tells us much about the Reformation in a Rhineland city, an area that research and standard treatments often neglect in favor of Zwinglian, Calvinist, and Lutheran centers. (Interestingly, however, traditions that benefited from Strasbourg's relative tolerance, even though they were elsewhere "ignored or suppressed" — such as the Mennonites — hear a great deal about this reformation center.) For another, by tracing KSZ's life, McKee identifies a pattern that can be observed elsewhere in the Reformation, and that may prove to characterize many other reform movements as well: that of the relative tolerance of the first generation giving way to increasing intolerance in the second. By identifying this pattern, McKee is not simply responding to the present's "lively issues," but suggesting a subject for investigation in many kinds of pasts.

Moreover, McKee finds in KSZ a way of being firmly committed on certain issues while being extraordinarily open in others. This consisted in affirming theologically that " 'Jesus is the Christ and the Son of God, and therefore He alone is the only Savior,' " while sharing house, goods, time, and energy with all who, regardless of their particular theologies, had need. To be sure, such a combination of affirmation and openness might rank favorably with today's ecumenical ideal. But not entirely. McKee makes it clear that, for KSZ, holding to her central conviction "meant rejecting the teaching of the papal church."

I hope that these brief references to McKee and Norris are enough to indicate that, while they certainly write with current issues in mind, their findings are more than mirror images of contemporary concerns. I hope they show that attention to "ignored or suppressed" histories and attempts to avoid "geographic centrism, classism, ethno-centricism, sexism" are more than mere current agenda. Efforts in these directions, I think, can help move historiography toward greater temporal and spatial globality — even if only paradoxically, along the path of difference.

Still, let us not underestimate the depth of Richard Norris's concern. For him, a chief "task of the historian *qua* historian is so to *distance* the past as to provide it with a voice that it can employ to shout the historian down." When the principles affirm their intent to take difference and otherness seriously, Norris responds, "what more thoroughgoing 'other' is there than the past?" When Principles 12 and 13 emphasize repentance and overcoming prejudices, Norris de-clares that "[i]t is when the relics of the past politely decline to conform to a given set of presuppositions and prejudices . . . that the process of purification begins."

In light of this emphasis, it seems fair to acknowledge that the foregoing essays, so far as I can see, do not contain striking instances of the past shrugging "its shoulders with indifference" or offering "re-sistance to the historian's introduction of her own 'lively issues.' " While Principle 8 affirms that ecumenical historiography can "discover paral-lels in other times and places to contemporary concerns," it does not indicate that phenomena which display no clear parallels might also be unearthed — and that these might also be valuable. While Principle 7, as Norris asserts, presupposes a continuity between present and past, the existence of possible discontinuity is not clearly acknowledged.

These criticisms, in my judgment, suggest that the principles in their present form might be somewhat too invested in finding com-monality, and not quite open enough to wrestling with real difference. (However, I represent a tradition that emphasized difference; some study group members might disagree.) This judgment echoes a con-cern raised about Jeff Gros's original proposal. Perhaps, then, Prin-ciples 7 and 8, presently grouped under the heading "Principles of Commonality," might ideally be balanced by at least one "Principle of Difference," or rewritten to incorporate this emphasis.

Nevertheless, it is not immediately evident that greater attention to difference need subvert the quest for unity. For recurring tension between these contrasting emphases, as we have seen, is intrinsic to the ecumenical venture itself. Perhaps in a history that can move "by leaps and bounds, shifts, anticipations and retardations," greater wrestling with real diversity, rather than contradicting unity, can prod one to conceive unity somewhat differently.

Ultimately, I agree with Richard Norris that the globality, or unity, or universality, so central to ecumenical historiography "functions more to designate a hope than it does to name an 'outlook.'" Such terms can no more denote a completed, objective perspective than can "all who call themselves Christians" constitute a final, fully adequate definition of this historiography's subject matter. Yet ecumenical historiographers, I think, still search for unity amid the vastly divergent expressions of what people call "Christian," and for unity of a global character despite the many divisive conflicts of our age, because they believe that these are real despite contrary appearances. However, this reality, as Gassmann points out, is "not simply and always a historical reality." Its ultimate character, that is, is eschatological, which means that certain of its characteristics may not yet fully exist as such. But if this unity is not yet fully present in all its dimensions, no one can now be certain which kinds of difference it may or may not embrace. In the meantime, the fourteen principles, however much eventual refinement they may need, provide promising tools for opening up and reevaluating what kinds of difference and commonality have existed in the past.

8. The Historiography of Christianity in Ecumenical Perspective: A Bibliographic Essay

Douglas A. Foster

Though this essay is modest, its goals are not. Its first aim is to point church historians, ecumenists, and others to a variety of examples of this volume's principles. It seeks to identify important efforts to tell untold stories — some of which may be unknown to all but ecumenical insiders. Together these studies show how ecumenical church history can and should be done, and they will, I hope, inspire others to do it, too.

A second objective is to promote a new concept of the teaching of church history at every level. The suggested sources of material and categories are for use in constructing new and renewed church history courses. Those who have worked on the project from which this volume issued are struggling toward creation of a more nearly complete picture of the church's history. This volume and this essay aspire to be a beginning place for many others to join in that task.

Two caveats. First, this essay is merely suggestive, not exhaustive. The initial concept for it included a massive survey of church history materials produced during the twentieth century and uncovered a vast amount of material. Yet no single organizational principle proved satisfactory for sorting and categorizing it. In the final analysis, the fourteen principles of ecumenical church history served as the primary organizational framework, though I have also

121

suggested an alternate approach that will uncover items not readily apparent in the first.

Second, this is not a bibliography of the history of the ecumenical movement. Although some materials included fit that category, they are here because of their relevance to ecumenical church history as defined in the fourteen principles.

General Materials

Before listing illustrations of specific ecumenical church history principles, I have several items of general importance to note. A multivolume work on Latin American church history served as a model of many of the ideals we seek to promote. Formed in 1972, the Study Commission on the History of the Church in Latin America (CE-HILA), coordinated by Enrique Dussel, has begun a project to tell the story of Latin American Christianity that includes the ideas and experiences of Latin Americans in light of their own contexts. The Commission's meetings have produced volumes that show the painstaking process by which this massive effort is being carried out and that lay the foundation for historical and theological work even beyond the initial project. The first meeting, in Quito in 1973, produced *Para Una Historia de la Iglesia en America Latina* (Toward a history of the church in Latin America),[1] which deals with methodological and historiographical question concerning a new Latin American church history. The third meeting, in Santo Domingo in 1975, produced *Para Una Historia de la Evangelizacion en America Latina* (Toward a history of the evangelization of Latin America), which proposes a chronological rather than geographical (country by country) approach to Latin American church history and gives a detailed proposal for the sixteenth through the eighteenth centuries. The eighth meeting, in Lima in 1980, resulted in the volume *Materiales Para una Historia de la Teologia en America Latina* (Materials for a history of theology in Latin America). All the volumes contain extensive bibliographies.

In the first volume of the projected eleven-volume church history,

---

1. Full publication information for works cited in this chapter is given in the last section, "Bibliography of Works Cited."

Dussel explains the theory behind the project. "This history intends to relate the life, the biography of the church, to remind it of its actions in favor of the poor and at the same time its complicity with the powerful. It will exalt her merits, but it will not hide her sins."[2] After volume 1 the books are organized geographically. Volumes in print as this essay is being prepared include volume 7, Colombia and Venezuela, 1981; volume 5, Mexico, 1984; volume 6, Central America, 1985; and volume 8, Peru, Bolivia, and Ecuador, 1987. Jeff Gros has written an excellent evaluation of the project in English.[3] An English translation of Dussel's earlier volume, *A History of the Church in Latin America: Colonialism to Liberation,* embodies the ideals seen in the CEHILA Spanish-language material.

In addition to the CEHILA project, two ground-breaking studies edited by Lukas Vischer deserve attention. The first is, as its subtitle indicates, a collection of the papers and reports of an International Ecumenical Consultation, held at Basel, October 12-17, 1981. It is titled *Church History in an Ecumenical Perspective.* It begins with a significant essay titled "Church History in an Ecumenical Perspective," followed by Vischer's study of the ecumenical significance of the Council of Basel. Five papers grouped under the heading "Towards a History of the Whole Church — New Horizons" deal with new approaches to church history in Latin America, the Pacific, India, and Africa, ending with a proposal for a new social history model to do church history.

The second volume, *Towards a History of the Church in the Third World: Papers and Report of a Consultation on the Issue of Periodisation,* came out of the meeting of the working Commission on Church History of the Ecumenical Association of Third World Theologians in 1983. The impetus behind this group has been to refocus church history in the so-called Third World away from the missionary venture and toward the experience of those who received and experienced the gospel. This volume proposes a periodization for church history based

2. Enrique D. Dussel, *Historia General de la Iglesia en America Latina,* Tomo I/1, *Introducción General a la Historia de la Iglesia en America Latina* (Salamanca: Ediciones Sigueme [for CEHILA], 1983).

3. Jeff Gros, "Interpretation, History, and the Ecumenical Movement," *Ecumenical Trends* 16 (July/August 1987).

on those churches' experiences. Six historians from different continents and countries did case studies for their own situation, then the consultation proposed an organization into five periods: before 1500, 1500-1800, 1800-1880, 1880-1945, and 1945-present. The group saw its work as "a necessary step towards a possible writing of a truly universal Church History from an ecumenical point of view."

Two important articles are found in the volume edited by Samuel Amirtham and Cyris H. S. Moon, *The Teaching of Ecumenics*. The first, an essay by T. V. Philip titled "Church History in Ecumenical Perspective," carefully contrasts the ecumenical perspective with other approaches to doing church history. The report of a working group on church history, titled "Teaching Church History from an Ecumenical Perspective," provides further clarification of the terms and their implications for church history. It ends with a suggested course outline for ecumenical church history and a brief but helpful bibliography.

Finally, in this category of general materials I call attention to Justo L. González's "Globalization in the Teaching of Church History." In this article Professor González, contributor of the Foreword to our volume, discusses the problem of even defining globalization, reviews five standard church history texts that seek to practice globalization, shares his own experience in trying to apply globalization to the work of the church historian, and offers the profile of a syllabus for an introductory course on church history.

Materials Illustrative of the Fourteen Principles

The fourteen principles are not discrete categories of literature. Some lend themselves more readily to specific illustration than do others. While some of the studies cited below could fit more than one of the principles, some of the principles are difficult to illustrate. There are some gaps — a need for examples — that the reader or teacher needs to help fill. Taken together, however, the following works point to the kind of church history we are aiming for.

The first principle states that ecumenical church history seeks to include in the story of Christianity all who call *themselves* Christians, including those marginalized in relation to the mainstream. Donald W.

Dayton's article "Yet Another Layer of the Onion: Or Opening the Ecumenical Door to Let the Riffraff In" speaks to the acceptance of religious outsiders, particularly focusing on evangelicals and Pentecostals.

Among materials that are global in outlook (though not necessarily in scope) are several significant projects seeking to tell the story of church history from the view of peoples not traditionally considered central to the story: Ogba Kalu, "African Church Historiography: An Ecumenical Perspective"; Jeffrey Klaiber, "Toward a New History of the Church in the Third World"; A. Mathias Mundadan, "Six Volume Project of Church History Association of India" (this article details the project that has resulted so far in three volumes of a *History of Christianity in India,* published in Bangalore by Theological Publications in India); H. D. Perumalil and Edward R. Hambye, eds., *Christianity in India: A History in Ecumenical Perspective.*

Diverse concepts of Christian identity and the location of apostolicity are the focus of a number of works issuing from the Apostolic Faith studies conducted by the National Council of Churches' Faith and Order group during the 1988 to 1991 quadrennium. Among those are S. Mark Heim, ed., *Faith to Creed: Toward a Common Historical Approach to the Affirmation of the Common Apostolic Faith in the Fourth Century;* Thaddeus D. Horgan, ed., *Apostolic Faith in America;* David T. Shannon and Gayraud S. Wilmore, eds., *Black Witness to the Apostolic Faith.* Another important work emphasizing commonalities in the midst of diversity is John Deschner et al., *Our Common History as Christians.*

Materials that investigate the relation between gospel, Christian communities, and culture include Howard Clark Kee et al., *Christianity: A Social and Cultural History;* Patricia Ruth Hill, *The World Their Household: The American Woman's Foreign Mission Movement and Cultural Transformation, 1870-1920;* Robert Wuthnow, *The Struggle for America's Soul: Evangelicals, Liberals, and Secularism.*

The area of the history of worship, piety, practice, and teaching, as well as the doctrine, history, and institutional development of the traditions, is vast. A basic dictionary of materials is J. D. Douglas, *The Concise Dictionary of the Christian Tradition: Doctrine, Liturgy, History.* A brief collection concerning development of black worship styles is Emmanual L. McCall, *Black Church Life-Styles.* Noteworthy also is

Herman A. J. Wegman, *Christian Worship in East and West: A Study Guide to Liturgical History.* Particularly significant on the development of American Protestant worship is James F. White, *Protestant Worship: Traditions in Transition.*

Materials that use "nontraditional" sources for historical analysis such as iconography, liturgy and worship, oral tradition, tracts and popular literature, and the archeological record are becoming more abundant: Moshe Barasch, *Icon: Studies in the History of an Idea;* John McRay, *Archaeology and the New Testament;* Eunice Dauterman McQuire, *Art and Holy Powers in the Early Christian House;* W. H. C. Frend, *Archaeology and History in the Study of Early Christianity.*

We are seeking materials that acknowledge that each generation and tradition understands the past in terms of its own issues and context: Jerald C. Brauer, ed., *Reinterpretation in American Church History;* Peter W. Williams, *America's Religions: Traditions to Denominations;* Peter A. Russell, "The Challenge of Writing Christian History."

We seek materials that discover parallels in other times and places to contemporary concerns to reexamine divisive issues: F. Forrester Church and Timothy George, eds., *Continuity and Discontinuity in Church History: Essays Presented to George Hunston Williams;* Nina G. Garsoian, "Byzantine Heresy: A Reinterpretation"; R. T. Beckwith, "The Office of Woman in the Church to the Present Day"; Janette Hassey, *No Time for Silence: Evangelical Women in Public Ministry Around the Turn of the Century;* William R. Farmer and Roch Kereszty, *Peter and Paul in the Church of Rome: The Ecumenical Potential of a Forgotten Perspective.*

We seek materials that help groups of Christians to define their own voices within the conversations among communities of faith and to issue their special challenge to these communities: Melanie A. May, *Women and Church: The Challenge of Solidarity in an Age of Alienation* and *Bonds of Unity: Women, Theology and the World-wide Church;* Sarah F. Anders, "Role of Women in American Religion"; Lois A. Boyd, *Presbyterian Women in America: Two Centuries of a Quest for Status;* Betty A. DeBerg, *Ungodly Women: Gender and the First Wave of American Fundamentalism;* Mary L. Hammack, *A Dictionary of Women in Church History;* Rosemary Radford Ruether and Rosemary Skinner Keller, eds., *Women and Religion in America* and *Women in*

Church History; Roger D. Hatch, "Integrating the Issue of Race into the History of Christianity in America"; Albert J. Raboteau, *Slave Religion: The "Invisible Institution" in the Antebellum South.*

We seek materials that open traditions to critical analysis by others, that help groups see themselves in a larger context and yet see their own unique strengths *and* that allow outsiders to analyze them critically.

We seek materials that welcome people to investigate with the historian the Christian past in a spirit of hospitality, that are accessible to nonspecialists/nonmembers of a particular tradition. A particularly fine example of this is Bruce L. Shelley, *Church History in Plain Language.*

We seek materials that approach their task in the spirit of repentance and forgiveness, avoiding defensiveness in regard either to social location or to particular theological, methodological, or ecclesial traditions.

We seek materials that understand and clearly acknowledge their own presuppositions and seek to overcome their prejudices.

We seek materials that acknowledge that no historical account can claim complete objectivity, but strive for fair-minded empathy with the particular stories that make up the ecumenical history of the Christian people.

An Alternate Approach and Some Sources of Materials

As mentioned, categorizing materials by the fourteen principles may leave out items valuable for constructing an ecumenical church history. A list of discrete subject categories might lend itself more readily to searches in the data bases suggested below. O. C. Edwards in his essay "Walker's Fourth Edition as Ecumenical History" (a report of the work done by the Faith and Order church history committee in evaluating the widely used Williston Walker church history text in light of the ecumenical church history principles) suggests the following categories as critical for doing church history ecumenically: (1) the role of laity in the church; (2) the role of women; (3) the role of the oppressed and persecuted; (4) the development of polity; (5) manifestations of the Spirit; (6) monasticism in relation to dualism and the imperial church; (7) the imperial church and its attempt at uniformity; (8) missiology; (9) non-Western churches or traditions; and (10) ethnic minorities. Under some of the headings a number of subgroups could be listed, for example, Latin America, Africa, and Asia under non-Western churches.

Sources of information about materials dealing with these and other topics important to this project are widely available. Copies of publications catalogs are available from the World Council of Churches (WCC Distribution Center, P.O. Box 346, Route 222 and Sharadin Road, Kutztown, PA 19530-0346) and the National Council of Churches (475 Riverside Drive, New York, NY 10115-0050). Four important journals whose articles and reviews will be increasingly important for this ecumenical effort are (1) the World Council of Churches' *Ecumenical Review,* (2) Graymoor Institute's *Ecumenical Trends* (Garrison, NY 10524), (3) the *Journal of Ecumenical Studies,* which is affiliated with the North American Academy of Ecumenists (NAAE, The Reverend Eugene L. Zoeller, Bellarmine College, Newburg Road, Louisville, KY 40205-0671), and (4) *International Christian Digest,* published by the United Methodist Publishing House, Nashville, TN.

Religion Index One and *Two,* produced by the American Theological Librarians Association, cover journal articles and books respectively. The indexes are available in printed form as well as in computer searchable format — CD-ROM — which is unbelievably fast, comprehensive, and up-to-date. Another prime source of information on journal articles is *Religious and Theological Abstracts,* again available in both printed form and on CD-ROM. Using key words from the lists above in combination with such words as "church history," "ecumenical," and "historiography," a researcher can find literally thousands of sources. Not all will be appropriate for illustrating the principles, so selectivity will be unavoidable. *Religious and Theological Abstracts,* however, gives the basic information contained in each article.

Access to the OCLC (On-Line Computing Library Center) database through a university or other library offers the capability to search under subject headings. Not all members of OCLC subscribe to that service, however. This is the largest Union Catalog in existence and will locate materials and allow for interlibrary loan requests through proper channels.

As I close this essay, let me issue one more word of warning. Trying to do church history ecumenically poses practical problems. Integration of the strands (social, cultural, institutional, theological, geographical, etc.) is sometimes difficult. Materials currently available are often narrowly focused. How can we put together the puzzle in a coherent way? For example, on the surface, treatments like Alec Vidler's *The Church in an Age of Revolution* and McLeod's *Religion and the People of Western Europe* seem to be looking at two completely different times and places! Melding and harmonizing the two borders on the impossible. Teachers, students, and ecumenists will find other instances of this problem in their work. While constructing a truly ecumenical approach to church history is a formidable task, it is work that must proceed, difficult or not. It may be that the simple telling of the stories without attempting to completely integrate them is the best initial approach.

This volume seeks to model how to do church history ecumenically. Its thesis is that every group, however defined, should tell its own story, and that all must listen to that story in an empathetic yet informed manner. It is our belief that this process can foster understanding, lessen contention, break down barriers, and promote Christian unity. The question now is, will it? It is truly all up to you.

Bibliography of Works Cited

Amirtham, Samuel, and Cyris H. S. Moon, eds. *The Teaching of Ecumenics.* Geneva: WCC Publications, 1987.

Anders, Sarah F. "Role of Women in American Religion." *Southwestern Journal of Theology* 18 (Spring 1976): 51-61.

Barasch, Moshe. *Icon: Studies in the History of an Idea.* New York: New York University Press, 1992.

Beckwith, Roger T. "The Office of Woman in the Church to the Present Day." *Why Not: Priesthood and Ministry of Women,* 26-39. Ed. M. Bruce. Appleford: Marchaw Manor Press, 1972.

Boyd, Lois A. *Presbyterian Women in America: Two Centuries of a Quest for Status.* Westport, CT: Greenwood Press, 1988.

Brauer, Jerald C., ed. *Reinterpretation in American Church History.* Chicago: University of Chicago Press, 1968.

CEHILA. *Materiales Para una Historia de la Teologia en America Latina* (Materials for a history of theology in Latin America). San Jose, Costa Rica: CEHILA, n.d.

———. *Para Una Historia de la Evangelizacion en America Latina* (Toward a history of the evangelization of Latin America). Barcelona: Editorial Nova Terra, 1977.

———. *Para Una Historia de la Iglesia en America Latina* (Toward a history of the church in Latin America). Barcelona: Editorial Nova Terra, 1975.

Church, F. Forrester, and Timothy George, eds. *Continuity and Discontinuity in Church History: Essays Presented to George Hunston Williams.* Leiden: E. J. Brill, 1979.

Dayton, Donald W. "Yet Another Layer of the Onion: Or Opening the Ecumenical Door to Let the Riffraff In." *The Ecumenical Review* 40 (January 1988): 88.

DeBerg, Betty A. *Ungodly Women: Gender and the First Wave of American Fundamentalism.* Minneapolis: Fortress Press, 1990.

Deschner, John, et al. *Our Common History as Christians.* Oxford: Oxford University Press, 1975.

Douglas, J. D. *The Concise Dictionary of the Christian Tradition: Doctrine, Liturgy, History.* Grand Rapids: Regency Reference Library, 1989.

Dussel, Enrique. *A History of the Church in Latin America: Colonialism to Liberation.* Grand Rapids: Eerdmans, 1981.

Edwards, O. C. "Walker's Fourth Edition as Ecumenical History." *Summary of Proceedings of the American Theological Librarians Association (ATLA)* 44 (1990): 257-64.

Farmer, William R., and Roch Kereszty. *Peter and Paul in the Church of Rome: The Ecumenical Potential of a Forgotten Perspective.* Mahwah, NJ: Paulist Press, 1990.

Frend, W. H. C. *Archaeology and History in the Study of Early Christianity.* London: Variorum Reprints, 1988.

Garsoïan, Nina G. "Byzantine Heresy: A Reinterpretation." *Dumbarton Oaks Paper: #25,* 85-113. Ed. George Ostrogorsky. Washington, DC: Dumbarton Oaks Center for Byzantine Studies, 1971.

González, Justo L. "Globalization in the Teaching of Church History." *Theological Education* 29, no. 2 (Spring 1993): 49-71.

Hammack, Mary L. *A Dictionary of Women in Church History*. Chicago: Moody Press, 1984.

Hassey, Janette. *No Time for Silence: Evangelical Women in Public Ministry Around the Turn of the Century*. Grand Rapids: Academic Books, 1986.

Hatch, Roger D. "Integrating the Issue of Race into the History of Christianity in America." *Journal of the American Academy of Religion* 46 (December 1978): 545-69.

Heim, S. Mark, ed. *Faith to Creed: Toward a Common Historical Approach to the Affirmation of the Common Apostolic Faith in the Fourth Century*. Grand Rapids: Eerdmans for the Commission on Faith and Order, NCCCUSA, 1991.

Hill, Patricia Ruth. *The World Their Household: The American Woman's Foreign Mission Movement and Cultural Transformation, 1870-1920*. Ann Arbor: University of Michigan Press, 1985.

Horgan, Thaddeus D., ed. *Apostolic Faith in America*. Grand Rapids: Eerdmans for the Commission on Faith and Order, NCCCUSA, 1988.

Kalu, Ogba, ed. *African Church Historiography: An Ecumenical Perspective*. Bern: Evangelische Arbeitsstelle Oekumene Schweiz, 1988.

Kee, Howard Clark, et al. *Christianity: A Social and Cultural History*. Columbus, OH: Macmillan Publishing Company, 1991.

Klaiber, Jeffrey. "Toward a New History of the Church in the Third World." *International Bulletin of Missionary Research* 14.3 (July 1990): 105-8.

May, Melanie A. *Bonds of Unity: Women, Theology and the World-wide Church*. Atlanta: Scholars Press, 1989.

——. *Women and Church: The Challenge of Solidarity in an Age of Alienation*. Grand Rapids: Eerdmans for the NCCCUSA, 1991.

McCall, Emmanual L. *Black Church Life-Styles*. Nashville: Broadman Press, 1986.

McRay, John. *Archaeology and the New Testament*. Grand Rapids: Baker Book House, 1991.

McQuire, Eunice Dauterman. *Art and Holy Powers in the Early Christian House*. Urbana: University of Illinois Press, 1989.

Mundadan, A. Mathias. "Six Volume Project of Church History Association of India." *East Asia Journal of Theology* 4 (1986): 175-77.

Perumalil, H. D., and Edward R. Hambye, eds. *Christianity in India: A History in Ecumenical Perspective*. Alleppy: Prakasam Publications, 1972.

Raboteau, Albert J. *Slave Religion: The "Invisible Institution" in the Antebellum South*. New York: Oxford University Press, 1978.

Ruether, Rosemary Radford, and Rosemary Skinner Keller, eds. *Women and Religion in America*. 3 vols. San Francisco: Harper and Row, 1981, 1985, 1986.

——, eds. *Women in Church History*. Austin, TX: Austin Presbyterian Theological Seminary, 1988.

Russell, Peter A. "The Challenge of Writing Christian History." *Fides et Historia* 21 (January 1989): 8-19.

Shannon, David T., and Gayraud S. Wilmore, eds. *Black Witness to the Apostolic Faith*. Grand Rapids: Eerdmans, 1985.

Shelley, Bruce L. *Church History in Plain Language*. Waco, TX: Word Books, 1982.

Vischer, Lukas, ed. *Church History in an Ecumenical Perspective*. Bern: Evangelische Arbeitsstelle Oekumene Schweiz, 1982.

——, ed. *Towards a History of the Church in the Third World: Papers and Report of a Consultation on the Issue of Periodisation*. Bern: Evangelische Arbeitsstelle Oekumene Schweiz, 1985.

Wegman, Herman A. J. *Christian Worship in East and West: A Study Guide to Liturgical History*. New York: Pueblo Publishing Company, 1985.

White, James F. *Protestant Worship: Traditions in Transition*. Louisville: Westminster/John Knox Press, 1989.

Williams, Peter W. *America's Religions: Traditions to Denominations*. Columbus, OH: Macmillan Publishing Company, 1990.

Wuthnow, Robert. *The Struggle for America's Soul: Evangelicals, Liberals, and Secularism*. Grand Rapids: Eerdmans, 1989.

Contributors to This Study

Members of the Apostolic Faith–History Committee of the Working Group on Faith and Order, National Council of the Churches of Christ in the USA, 1988-1991

(In deference to those whose responsibilities prohibited active participation, this is not a complete roster of the Committee.)

Craig Atwood, Pastor of the Moravian Church in America, Philadelphia, Pennsylvania.

Paul M. Bassett, Professor of the History of Christianity, Nazarene Theological Seminary, Kansas City, Kansas.

Charles W. Brockwell, Jr., Director of Graduate Studies and Professor of Church History & Wesley Studies, Louisville Presbyterian Theological Seminary, Louisville, Kentucky.

Donald Bruggink, Professor of Historical Theology, Western Theological Seminary, Holland, Michigan.

David E. Daniels, Assistant Professor of Church History, McCormick Theological Seminary, Chicago, Illinois.

Donald Dayton, Professor of Theology and Ethics, Northern Baptist Theological Seminary, Lombard, Illinois.

O. C. Edwards, Jr. (chair, 1990-91), Professor of Preaching, Seabury-Western Theological Seminary, Evanston, Illinois.

Thomas Finger, Professor of Systematic and Spiritual Theology, Eastern Mennonite Seminary, Harrisonburg, Virginia.

Douglas A. Foster, Associate Professor of Church History and Director of the Center for Restoration Studies, Abilene Christian University, Abilene, Texas.

Paul Gritz, Associate Professor of Church History, Southwestern Baptist Theological Seminary, Ft. Worth, Texas.

S. Mark Heim, Professor of Christian Theology, Andover Newton Theological School, Newton Centre, Massachusetts.

Rosemary Jermann, co-editor of *Theology Digest* and Adjunct Instructor of Theological Studies, St. Louis University, St. Louis, Missouri.

James Jorgenson, Associate Professor of Church History, Sacred Heart Major Seminary, Detroit, Michigan.

Elizabeth H. Mellon (staff), Associate Director, Graymoor Ecumenical Institute, New York, New York.

Lauree Hersch Meyer (chair, 1988-89), Director of the Continuing Education and Doctor of Ministry Programs, Associate Professor of Theology, Colgate Rochester Divinity School/Bexley Hall/Crozer Theological Seminary, Rochester, New York.

Samuel Nafzger, Executive Director, Lutheran Church–Missouri Synod Commission on Theology & Church Relations, St. Louis, Missouri.

Frederick W. Norris, Professor of Christian Doctrine, Emmanuel School of Religion, Johnson City, Tennessee.

William G. Rusch, Director, Department for Ecumenical Affairs, Evangelical Lutheran Church of America, Chicago, Illinois.

Timothy J. Wengert, Associate Professor of the History of Christianity, Lutheran Theological Seminary, Philadelphia, Pennsylvania.

Scholars Invited by the Commission to Share in the Project

Roberta C. Bondi, Professor of Church History, Candler School of Theology, Emory University, Atlanta, Georgia.

Günther Gassmann, Executive Secretary, Commission on Faith and Order, World Council of Churches, Geneva, Switzerland.

Justo L. González, Director, The Hispanic Summer Program, Fund for Theological Education, Decatur, Georgia.

James Hennesey, S.J., Professor of Church History, Canisius College, Buffalo, New York.

Elsie Anne McKee, Archibald Alexander Associate Professor of the History of Worship, Princeton Theological Seminary, Princeton, New Jersey.

Richard A. Norris, Professor of Church History, Union Theological Seminary, New York, New York.

Paulo Siepierski, Professor of Church History, Semmario Theologico do Norte do Brazil, Recife, Brazil.